IMPRESSIONS OF SELF

A FRAMEWORK FOR BUILDING
SELF-ESTEEM

Dennis C. Westin, M.D.

Order this book online at www.trafford.com
or email orders@trafford.com

Most Trafford titles are also available at major online book retailers.

Printed in the United States of America.

ISBN: 978-1-4269-6830-3 (sc)
ISBN: 978-1-4269-6831-0 (hc)
ISBN: 978-1-4269-6832-7 (e)

Library of Congress Control Number: 2011907874

Trafford rev. 11/16/2011

 www.trafford.com

North America & international
toll-free: 1 888 232 4444 (USA & Canada)
phone: 250 383 6864 ♦ fax: 812 355 4082

Table of Contents

Above all, guard
your heart for it is the
wellspring of life.

Proverbs 4:23

INTRODUCTION

After more than 25 years of psychiatric practice, with a little general medicine thrown in, I've been impressed by the prevalence of problems that severely affect our thoughts, feelings, and behaviors—impressed by the vastness of similarities between us as well as the vastness of differences—impressed by the body's (a unified mind/body) flexibility to tolerate and deal with physical and mental stress, and impressed by the same body's "limits" of flexibility and tolerance.

Over and over again, I have looked for a common root of problems—tried to identify a beginning point, or at least a major element of a problem that could be focused on—the one thing that could make the most difference if changed—the one thing that you can influence that will keep you on your road of life and make the trip more peaceful.

That one thing, I believe, is self-esteem—your **impressions of self**.

You can feel better, enjoy life more, and experience more inner peace if you have a solid, positive, feeling about yourself. You can gain more positive impressions of self if you are not afraid to be **aware of yourself**, the good and the bad, and to **invest energy** into being the kind of person you really want to be.

Too often you may look on such a challenge as impossible.

In the following pages you will see that there is not only hope, there is the ability within you to develop and maintain a comfortable, invigorating, productive self-esteem that can help keep you on life's road of unexpected twists and turns—a self-esteem that can help you feel inner peace and share that inner peace with others.

These pages do not hold all the answers, but they do contain enough guidelines to help you begin your journey and to help you develop your own positive course. They can show you how to create your own personal, expanded guidelines that can give you a positive, healthy direction throughout your life.

I have tried to make these guidelines specific and understandable, using repetition to help reinforce concepts and suggestions. My intent has been to do that in a relatively short number of pages so you can read it easily and then go back and read it again. The first seven chapters tell you what self-esteem is and how you can take charge of the changes you want to make to help build positive self-esteem. The last seven chapters deal with specific areas of change, "rules" for self that, I believe, will strengthen your positive self-esteem. I would suggest that you read through all chapters first and then go back and spend more time on each one.

As a medical student making rounds with attending physicians or being in class, we would be given short statements of advice/ wisdom, called "Pearls." At the end of each chapter is a summary of important points from that chapter, also entitled "Pearls." Following the Pearls is a short list of "Considerations." These are activities you can consider doing to better understand and use the information in the chapter.

Before you begin, think of how you rate your self-esteem. Give it a number from 1 to 10, where 1 is the lowest level of self-esteem and 10 is the highest. Also, using the same number system, rate how sure you are about your self-esteem "number." When you have completed the changes in habits suggested in this book, go through the self-esteem rating process again and see if the numbers have changed.

Allow yourself to focus on the content of these pages—let it sink in and become a comfortable, positively stimulating part of your very own **impressions of self**.

Have a successful, gratifying journey.

Dennis

CHAPTER 1

UNDERSTANDING SELF-ESTEEM

Before you can really focus and learn, you need to understand what the focus is. Therefore, I think you should look at how you might define "self-esteem."

To me, self-esteem is how you view yourself from all angles—how you think about yourself, feel about yourself, how you see yourself "in your mind's eye"—your total impression of self.

If you look in Webster's Collegiate Dictionary, you will see that there can be a problem with defining self-esteem. This is evident in the definition itself, which is as follows: "(1) belief in one's self; self-respect, (2) undue pride in one's self; conceit."

Which way do you go with this definition?

Unfortunately, some people are taught that thinking about one's self and looking at self is "selfish." Therefore, it is undesirable, even "evil," "bad" and "prideful," as in Webster's second definition. Such thinking stimulates the creation and growth of poor self-esteem and **resistance** to positive change in self-esteem.

If that is your situation, are you comfortable with it?

Does this negative definition of self-esteem allow feelings that are positive, loving, caring and enduring?

Does such negatively defined self-esteem make it easier for you to interact on the "road of life" and experience joy, fulfillment, and inner peace?

I think you need to ask yourself if it is really "bad" to pay attention to self—to take positive care of self—to nurture self.

Unfortunately, you will get nowhere with positive change of self-esteem unless you really, deeply feel it is **okay** to make changes in yourself. You have to truly accept that it is **okay** to change in order to overcome the resistance, or barriers, blocking change in self—esteem.

Thus, for change to occur, you need to explore your thoughts and feelings in the "permission" area to see if it is **okay** for you to have **positive** impressions of self. **This is a very important point**.

Such "permission" or lack of "permission" often is hidden in the shadow of your thoughts and subtly influences what your mind does. You have to get beyond this point to have good self-esteem. The only way to get beyond it is to really ask yourself if it is **okay** for you to feel good about you, to have good thoughts, feelings or impressions about yourself.

If it's not okay—it won't work! Review this issue with yourself—do it several times, if necessary, until you know what your position is. It has to be **okay** to make positive changes in self to feel good, or it won't happen!

You will see more ways to deal with change in Chapter five.

Too often the "negatives" associated with self-esteem are taught to you as you grow up. This may have occurred in your home, in your school, in your place of worship, or in whatever place and with whatever people you spent a significant amount of time.

Religion sometimes conveys such negatives. In the Bible, not much is directly written about self-esteem. The Bible speaks of "pride," but in a negative way—such as "false pride," which is "bad." It encourages you to be "giving, loving, and patient" with others yet somehow lacks emphasis on the importance of also directing such desirable thoughts, feelings and behaviors toward yourself. At least, it does not appear to directly address that concept.

However, if you look more carefully and think more broadly, you will see another side to that—the side of the Bible that supports caring for self and having a positive, healthy impression of self.

The Bible tells you to take care of yourself—to see yourself as God's creation—and thus, to honor self as well as others.

It tells you to treat others as you would like to be treated. Don't you think most people would like to be treated fairly, with love, compassion, understanding, and trust? Wouldn't you like to be treated that way? Don't you think it's important to treat yourself that way?

So maybe the Biblical scripture does direct you to think about yourself, to **treat yourself fairly** with love, compassion, understanding, and trust—to give yourself **permission** to nurture and build a positive self-esteem. If you see yourself as God's creation, don't you have the responsibility and the right to take care of that creation—the responsibility to take care of yourself in a positive way?

In reading about Buddhism, you might find similar ideas—ideas stating that you have to let go of your worldly attachments to find "inner peace," i.e., Nirvana. In my view, that doesn't mean just making your worldly possessions less important. It means shifting your energy, focus, and nurturing from those external possessions to **enriching your inner self**.

Great Thinkers of the Eastern World, edited by Ian P. McGreal, Harper Collins Publishers, explains how Buddha (Siddhirtha Geuterma) acquired enlightenment and saw "the path that leads to the end of all suffering and to liberation (Nirvana) . . . Nirvana has been described as the Great Peace, perfection, extinction . . . The basic Buddhist precept was to consider all beings as like oneself." In so doing, Buddhists are to practice and develop "**friendliness, compassion, sympathetic joy and impartiality to others and to self.**" I interpret that to mean that it is **necessary** and **okay** to pay attention to your own thoughts, feelings and behaviors, and to do those things that will nurture your inner self in a positive, peaceful way.

I believe such a process will also improve and nurture your self-esteem.

Reportedly, Buddha found through his own experience that self torture and extreme self denial would never lead to "enlightenment," "Nirvana," or "peace." Thus he stopped self-punishment and went down a different road in search of inner peace.

You may have your own ways, whether small or large, of "torturing" and/or denying yourself. They may be physical and/or emotional. You have to become **aware** of these ways as they block the road to positive self-esteem—to peace in and with yourself. You need to identify those **barriers**, deal with them, and find another route to your inner peace, perhaps a more inner route.

Hinduism teaches that you continue to be reborn until you achieve "spiritual perfection."

One way Webster defines "spiritual" is as "the thinking, motivating, feeling part of man, often as distinguished by the body, mind, intelligence."

Thus, you would see **life's challenge as "perfecting" that "spiritual" part of yourself, that part where your thoughts and feelings reside and from which your behaviors are directed.**

I also see self-esteem being generated and fed, either positively or negatively, in this way. Thus, I believe the Hindu religion supports the need and permission to develop positive self-esteem, to take good care of your inner self. In so doing, you can find a more fulfilling life and greater inner peace. It also points out that doing so can take time.

Needless to say, there are always "extremes." On the whole, extremes are not desirable. You could say the extreme of positive self-esteem is conceit, narrow-minded self-centeredness, arrogance, and even "false pride."

That certainly is not what this book is encouraging, nor what would be considered healthy or what could result in true inner peace.

However, the other extreme is also unhealthy. Too often, in fact, this is where you might find yourself: at the extreme of strong dislike or even hate of self. The purpose of the following chapters is to help you move from the extremes, to help you find a more comfortable **middle ground** where you can live more peacefully with yourself and with life in this world.

Hopefully, the preceding information will help you feel that it's **okay** to pay attention to yourself—to **give** yourself **permission** to invest energy and time into **letting** your self-esteem be what you truly would like it to be.

Hopefully, you will help yourself learn to gain control over your thoughts, feelings and behaviors, and have that control result in positive outcomes.

No doubt the "forces" inside you, be they positive or negative, can be very strong and unrelenting.

And unfortunately, too often they are negative.

When a part of you knows you are good and deserving, and another part feels you are undeserving of love, acceptance, and fair treatment, a battle results—an inner battle or perhaps a spiritual battle.

Many of us are unwilling to **consciously** engage in such a "battle." Perhaps this is because we lack the energy or because we feel so undeserving of "good" for ourselves. Yet, I would bet that you do have times of feeling the discomfort from your inner "battle"—you are aware of a fight going on inside you and you want it resolved—you want peace.

The chapters ahead will offer suggestions to help you on your way. Just in case the above ideas are not enough to help you accept that having positive impressions of yourself is **okay** and indeed vital to peaceful survival on earth, you can look into the next chapter and learn more about the "importance" of positive self-esteem.

— —

<u>Pearls</u>:

1. Self-esteem is how you **think about, feel about and see yourself**—your total impressions of yourself.
2. Self-esteem can be defined positively or negatively— **it's up to you**.
3. All in all, I believe that various religions support the formation of good, positive self-esteem, although sometimes it doesn't appear that way.
4. I believe the location of self-esteem is also the location of one's spiritual self—that area inside where thoughts and feelings reside and from which your behaviors are directed.
5. To make changes to improve self-esteem, **it has to be okay** or change will not occur. You must honestly accept that it's **okay** to feel good about self—to see self in a positive way. That is the key that will unlock the door to change.

<u>Considerations</u>:

1. Define self-esteem—as you see it.
2. Describe your own self-esteem.
3. Where do you want your self-esteem to be on the self-esteem scale that we talked about in the Introduction?
4. Is there a battle going on within you regarding how "deserving" you are of good feelings? If so, be **aware** of that battle and the feelings and behaviors that go with it. Write down one of those battles where your thoughts are saying or implying it's not okay to feel good about yourself. Also write down how that makes you feel and behave.
5. Are you willing to be more aware of self? List three reasons why it's good to be more aware and three reasons that get in the way.
6. If you are religious, does your religion re-enforce your self-esteem or hinder it? Explain.

CHAPTER 2

IMPORTANCE OF SELF-ESTEEM

How do you feel when you are home alone or with family—when out in a crowd, at the grocery store, or at work?

How do you feel when you have to make decisions—when those decisions work out well, or when they don't work out well?

How do you feel when people disagree with you—when their response to you is negative?

How do you feel when faced with other stressful situations? Are they "threats" or are they "challenges and opportunities?"

How do you handle compliments? Do you truly accept them and let them sink in to nurture and strengthen your self-esteem? Do you automatically negate them with thoughts such as, "If they really knew me, they wouldn't say that," or "I really should have done better, so what they are saying really doesn't mean anything," or "They are just saying that to be nice?"

No doubt you can think of other similar situations where you basically "negate" yourself and those ideas that can help build a positive impression of yourself. These are situations where your poor self-esteem causes negative, bad, sad, anxious, and sometimes, unfortunately, self-destructive thoughts, feelings and behaviors.

At the **core** of your thoughts, feelings and behaviors is how you see yourself—your **self-esteem**.

How can you ever feel "good" and have peace within yourself if you can't basically like yourself, love yourself, have confidence in yourself, and have flexibility with all of those thoughts and feelings?

Too many people want perfection!

You have to accept that you won't be perfect. However, you can still strive to get as close as possible to your idea of perfection for yourself and, in the process, experience a preponderance of pleasure, satisfaction, and inner peace.

Self-esteem is the nucleus, the center of your world—the point around which your personal world revolves.

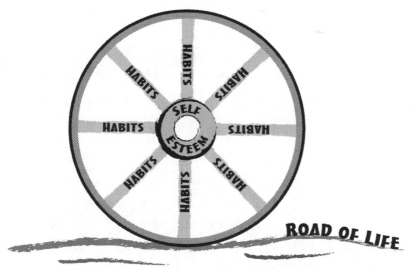

Self-esteem is like the **hub** of the wagon wheel; your habits of thinking, feeling and behaving, developed over the years, are like the spokes. If your self-esteem isn't positive, strong and reasonably steady because of too many negative habits, the hub will collapse and the multitude of spokes in your life will crumble and break; your trip on life's path will be mostly unpleasant and unsatisfactory. It will be filled with upheaval and trauma, lacking in peacefulness, and fulfillment.

Many people ask, "Why can't I cope with stress the way I used to? Why can't I be as helpful to others or as active in as many volunteer organizations? Why do the kids irritate me more? Why am I less tolerant of others' behaviors—spouses, friends, and fellow employees?" Have you ever asked these questions?

In these situations you no doubt feel a marked lack of gratification in your life and an increasing frustration with yourself. Although such thoughts and feelings can be the result of depression, anxiety, or highly stressful events in your life, they can also lead to anxiety, depression, phobias, and other undesirable emotional states.

Where does self-esteem fit in here?

Most likely, if you have a strong, positive impression of yourself and know how to keep that self-esteem growing, as you grow, you won't "wear out" in these ways. Those "spokes" of your life will be strong and will allow you to continue smoothly on your trip through life because your **hub**—your **nucleus**—your **self-esteem** is solid, reliable and **well cared for**.

Often you can get along life's path "okay" by learning to smile, or to be "agreeable." You learn to anticipate the needs of others so you can meet those needs and in so doing, feel you are doing what's "right" and what will bring you happiness, satisfaction, acceptance, and love. For a while all this works, and you don't feel a lot of emotional pain.

Eventually, however, you get tired of doing this; for whatever reason it just doesn't work anymore. You develop the awareness that these habits of thinking, feeling and behaving, learned in childhood and "refined" in your growing-up years, really aren't meeting your needs. You aren't feeling more secure within yourself. You aren't thinking you are more lovable and acceptable. In other words, these habits really haven't helped you obtain and maintain a positive, lasting impression of yourself.

If positive self-esteem had been more "solidly rooted" deep within you, you wouldn't be facing this predicament. Your nurturing would come **from within you where you have control, not from outside where you have limited or no control.**

How you think about yourself, how you feel about yourself, how you see yourself, the impressions you have of yourself, influence almost everything you think, do and feel. This is like the "filter" through which your experiences, decisions, and interpretations pass.

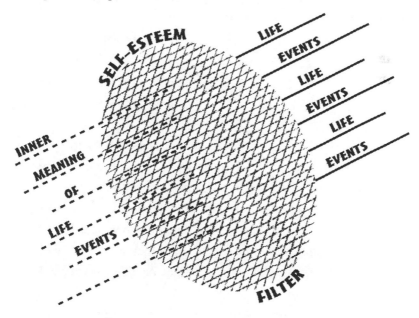

Isn't it most desirable to have a positive "filter," a strong one that keeps working for you throughout life? A filter that can block out the harshness of the negatives in life and let you see and experience the positives.

Wouldn't that increase your odds of more positive inner impressions, more happiness in life, more peacefulness, more clear thinking and objectivity?

Wouldn't you see that as very important, very desirable?

Not only is this desirable, it is obtainable; you **deserve it, right?**

Hopefully, the importance of self-esteem is getting clearer to you. No doubt, when you really think about it, you can see other factors that underscore the importance of positive impressions of self. These factors can help you stay "engaged" in the process of learning and maintaining a strong, positive, comfortable, and internally generated self-esteem.

To help you further understand self-esteem, you next need to consider where the self-esteem you now have came from—be it good or bad or somewhere in between. We will explore that topic in the next chapter.

Pearls:
1. See stressful, challenging situations as **opportunities, not threats.** They are opportunities to be more aware of self and help self be what you want to be.
2. The **core** or **hub** of your "wagon wheel" or of your being is your **self-esteem.** It depends on your habits of thinking, feeling and behaving which are the spokes that cause it to be able, or to not be able to carry the "weight" of life.
3. Ways of dealing with stress or negative situations, acquired at a young age, often don't work as we get older, yet they still influence us. That is because they

have become **habits** and the longer they go on, the less we are aware of them.

4. Self-esteem is also like a **filter** that influences how we see life and determines how we interpret and deal with our environment

Considerations:

1. What makes self-esteem important to you? List three reasons.

2. Is your self-esteem the "hub" of your "wheel?" Do you see it as a center of influence on your life? If so, in what way?

3. Do you see stressful situations as threats or opportunities? List two stressful situations and note how they could be threats and how they could be opportunities.

CHAPTER 3

DEVELOPMENT OF SELF-ESTEEM

Although I view the development of self-esteem as a continuous process, one that runs throughout life, I think the most powerful, influential period of that development is during our younger years. Some people steadfastly believe that **infancy** and **childhood experiences** have nothing to do with how we are today and how we will be tomorrow. However, I believe the majority of people accept the impact of those early influences on their lives and the continuing role they play throughout life.

Besides experiences, the **genetic factor** also influences you from the very beginning of your being. Just as these genetic factors establish your height, color of hair, eyes and skin, they also set the stage or build the framework on which and within which your self-esteem and personality develop.

You can see individuals who are calm, just like their mother or father or "Aunt Sue," and those that are explosive or easily agitated, just like other "biological relatives." The interplay of genetics and environmental factors becomes quite complex, and it is often hard to tell which came first, "the chicken or the egg." It's the "nature or nurture" question.

I believe you begin with the **genetic aspect** of self, and as you experience life, the **environmental influence produces habits that are wrapped around it**; much like thread is wrapped around a spool.

GENETICS

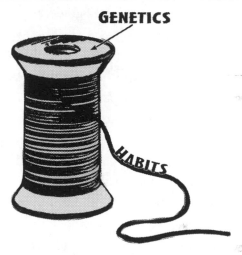

If you maintain flexible thinking, you will benefit by accepting that both genetics and your reaction to your environment are primary forces affecting development of self-esteem. Let's look at a fictional example.

Mary Ann is a 24-year-old woman who has been in an abusive relationship with her husband, George, for two years. He easily gets agitated, especially after his nightly intake of alcohol. He lashes out at her, yells at her, and demeans her physically and mentally.

They have a 4-year-old son and a 2-year-old daughter. Since Mary Ann thinks she has no profession or skills, and George makes a good salary at his job, she thinks it would be harder to leave him and support herself and their children than to stay and receive the abuse. She has no support system, such as good friends or dependable relatives, because she has always felt unworthy of friendship.

Mary Ann came from a family where drinking and violence were a daily part of life. Her parents both worked, so she, as the oldest, had to care for her younger brother and sister as well as clean the house and cook meals. Because of these responsibilities, she dropped out of school after the 8th grade. She felt no love, no acceptance, and no "joy" of childhood.

Regardless of how hard she tried to accomplish the chores and do them "super well," Mary Ann had the impression they were never done good enough for her parents. Her parents continued to complain and yell at her, as well as at each other.

She tried to protect her younger brother John, and her sister Amy, from their parents' abuse by putting herself between them and their parents, and by getting them to their rooms or out of the house when fights occurred.

Although, while she was still in school, Mary Ann had one friend, she was ashamed to have that friend over to her house because of her parents' behavior. She became quite isolated in that respect, and at an early age, she began to feel even more **unlovable** and **unacceptable**.

Maybe if she just worked harder, kept the kitchen cleaner, kept Johnny and Amy more quiet, and fixed better meals, her parents would be pleased with her and be kind to her, as well as to her brother and sister and each other. Maybe they would stop their fighting. Mary Ann felt a sense of responsibility for her parents' behavior and their perceived rejection of her.

In addition, people often told Mary Ann that she looked like her mother, was quiet, and was a hard worker like her mother. This wasn't especially pleasing to her, although at times she thought her mother was beautiful; at other times she felt her mother was very tired and too passive. As she began to see these characteristics in herself, Mary Ann became even more frustrated. She thought she had even more evidence for seeing herself negatively and as being unacceptable.

Unfortunately, too many people are in this kind of situation and have this kind of history. As you can imagine or as you may know, the feelings associated with such thoughts and experiences are very despairing and depressing.

It's very hard to imagine something different in life unless you have actually seen it yourself. If you can gather more hope and **better impressions of self**, you can then begin to imagine a **better life . . .** a **better way of existing.** You can imagine that life is not only a matter of simple existence—of putting one foot in front of the other—but it's more. It's living with a sense of purpose, accomplishment, and gratification.

As for Mary Ann, how would you view her self-esteem? How would you see that self-esteem when she was a child?

How do you rate Mary Ann's self-esteem as a child, as a young adult, and as a mother and wife?

Do you think Mary Anne's self-esteem may have been influenced by her genetics, her biological inheritance—or by her environment, her experiences in life?

In psychiatry, we see patients almost every day with such unfortunate histories. Although the one above is simplified, it represents how certain thoughts, feelings and behaviors are passed from generation to generation—through both genetics and environment.

We aren't born with the need for negative habits; negative thoughts, feelings or behavior.

We are all born with the need for love and acceptance! These are positives!

I tend to believe an unborn child can even detect the presence or absence of love. We know smoking and drug use can affect the unborn child, so why not the chemicals stimulated by its mother's emotions—chemicals associated with calm and love or chemicals associated with fear and anger?

How you start to view yourself—what **impression you have of yourself starts early**—very early!

If you tend to be "hyper" because of your genetics, and your environment responds to that with ridicule and anger, you either decide to work harder to get the approval or love you need, or you rebel and at least get attention that way.

In the process you are forming, in this case, negative impressions of yourself, negative habits. You think something must be wrong with you to "cause" such responses from others.

As an infant or child, you feel responsible for everything that happens in your "world" and believe that you can control your world. As a child you see everything around you as part of your world; truly, you are the center of it. Therefore, whatever happens to you or around you has to do with you; you feel a responsibility for it.

If your mother or father is angry, even if it is not directed at you, you feel you must have done something wrong that caused the anger. You might feel you are supposed to control the situation to avoid the anger. When the anger occurs anyway and you are unable to control your environment, you feel weak and ineffective. You think this means that you are bad and undeserving of your parents' love and acceptance.

Feeling bad makes you think you are undeserving of everyone else's love and acceptance.

This doesn't necessarily mean that you stop trying to get others' love and acceptance. Often, you keep trying, but unfortunately the "die has been cast" in regard to your self-esteem, and your sense of "worthiness" of anything good in life coming your way—just as with Mary Ann and her attempt to do everything just right in hopes of being loved and accepted.

You make many such decisions in your youth. Some are made very quickly—others more slowly.

Sometimes you have a brief awareness of these decisions; however, that soon turns to "unawareness" as it sinks into the subconscious or even the unconscious. At other times, you are entirely unaware of the whole process. You are just trying to survive the best you can.

Unless you become **aware** of those **habits of thoughts, feelings** and **behaviors** at some time in your life, you cannot change them. They will continue to determine your path in life based on these "early reactions and habits," and not based on your true desires for yourself.

When you make conscious or unconscious decisions about yourself at a very young age, **those decisions, thought habits, are usually reinforced as you get older.**

One could determine that Mary Ann, because of very low self-esteem influenced by her environment and genetics, chose a mate who continued to abuse her as she thought her parents had. No doubt, her thought was that this was not only the behavior she was used to, it was, unfortunately, what at least part of her felt she deserved. She also behaved in a more passive way with her husband as her mother had with Mary Ann's father.

In turn, her husband's abuse reinforced Mary Ann's sense of unworthiness and poor self-esteem and continued her sense of isolation. It also continued the environmental teaching cycle by showing her children that such behavior and low self-worth are acceptable. Other possible consequences of such behavior could be depression, anxiety, and substance abuse.

Thus, the **development of self-esteem is a process influenced by genetics and environment that begins at a very early point**

in life. It continues throughout life—whether you like it or not and whether you decide to influence it or not! Hopefully, you will become **aware and decide to influence your self-esteem in a positive way**.

I am writing much of this book only when I have free time, such as while taking a business trip or short vacation. At this particular moment, I'm sitting overlooking the beach at Puerto Penasco, Mexico. As I think about the development of self-esteem, I look at how that relates to the scene before me. Out on the Sea of Cortez, I see the shrimp boats that have come in from their night's fishing, the waves very gently washing up on the beach and the sands white and clear out to the blue horizon. About 75 yards up on the beach is an old rusted shrimp boat that appears to have been there for many years. Maybe I can draw some parallels between this scene and the development of our self-esteem.

I see the shrimp boats as they come into the bay, bringing food for those of us on shore. Although not too kind to the fish or shrimp, their harvest is nurturing to those who enjoy eating it and it provides sustenance for our bodies.

Likewise, experiences that feed our "souls" or our "hub" come into our lives. These experiences go to the inner part of our personal being, shaping and influencing it, forming habits of thinking, feeling and behaving.

As I see the waves gently lapping upon the sand, I observe how they leave an impression in the sand; much as do the experiences we have in our life. As they touch us, they also make an impression in the form of habits of thinking, feeling and behaving. When the tide moves in further, those impressions in the sand will be covered. Likewise, our experiences/habit formations are sometimes forgotten, at least at the conscious level; they sink down to a deeper level, a subconscious or unconscious level. On the upper level, our conscious level, the beach is clear, and more impressions can be made later, as the tide again moves the sand and leaves a new imprint.

Some or our experiences/habits are not so nice, like the wrecked, rusted shrimp boat up on the beach. They lie in our memory bank, at our unconscious or subconscious level. At times, they get in our way. They can cause bad feelings and bad behaviors. They can be "barriers" to learning good habits.

On a more personal note, I believe most of the habits you form as a reaction to your environment **are changeable**. **You can influence almost all of them**. You **can influence** your **interpretation** of your **nurturing or growing up years**. You **can influence** the **impressions** that events in life make upon your mind. You **can influence** the **impact** of the obstacles or barriers that life has put before you and within you. I'm not saying it's easy to do this, but I am saying it is usually possible.

Hopefully, as you read further, you will learn tools to help accomplish these tasks. In so doing, you can markedly improve the impressions you have of self.

You can shape yourself to be the kind of person you want to be!

Pearls:

1. The development of self-esteem results from **genetics** and **environment,** like threads (habits from reacting to our environment) wrapped around a spool (our genetics).

2. Formation of self-esteem starts as soon as our mind **senses** our environment and has to decide how to **react** to it. That reaction forms a habit of thinking, feeling and behaving. A habit "triad" that we will explore in the next chapter.

3. We can't change our genetics, but we **can** change how we let our environment influence us, and the habits we develop as a result.

4. Our reaction to our environment, or the people and situations around us, affects our thoughts, feelings and behaviors. It sets up habits that will affect us the rest of our lives, or at least until we become aware of them and change them.

Considerations:

1. Do you accept the idea that self-esteem starts very early in life?

2. If you accept it—why do you? If you don't, why not? Write a few sentences explaining your answer.

3. Can you understand that we develop habits of thinking, feeling and behaving in response to our environment? Explain why that seems reasonable or why it does not seem reasonable.

4. Do you think you have power, influence and control over how you respond to, and especially "interpret" the events in your environment? Write down reasons and examples for your response.

CHAPTER 4

BAD HABITS OF SELF-ESTEEM & THE HABIT TRIAD

I always feel sad seeing the adult or child who didn't really have the opportunity to develop positive **impressions of self**. On the other hand, it is enjoyable and refreshing to see those who think well of themselves—who were shown how and were encouraged to see themselves positively—who felt love and acceptance and were spared the heaviness and pain of significant self-doubt in those early "impressionable" years of growing up. It reminds me of one of the license plate choices here in Arizona that reads, "It shouldn't hurt to be a child."

Although those with good, comfortable self-esteem are not really the focus of these writings, I at least want to acknowledge their existence and the positive influence they have on life. They show us that such positive **impressions of self** are indeed possible and can be enjoyable and refreshing to one's self and to others.

Even if you didn't develop enough positive habits or positive self-esteem in your earlier life, you **can make changes** as your life goes on.

In Mary Ann's story, we saw how she developed **bad habits of self-esteem**. She developed the belief-habit of thinking she was unlovable, unacceptable, not as "good" as others, not as "deserving" as others. This unhealthy habit then encouraged more negative thinking about herself and led to sad, hurt feelings and behaviors that she didn't feel good about.

With such a collection of habits, she and others with comparable early beginnings become extremely efficient at picking up the "negative" in situations and ignoring or not even seeing the "positive."

The **basis for interpreting life events, or their "filter," then becomes negative**.

This only encourages more negativity and lowered self-esteem. You need to be **aware** of your habits and self-esteem so you can make the necessary changes in them—so you can become more like the person you want to be.

Let's look at a few negative habits of self-esteem:

1. Seeing self as **"less" than others**—not as good, not as talented, not as intelligent, not as athletic or coordinated, not as pretty or thin or muscular, not as good at making friends or socializing, not as happy. Comparing yourself to others often encourages these impressions. You will explore that habit more in Chapter 10.

2. Seeing mainly the **negative in situations** and self. This often originates from not having had the opportunity or "modeling" to see and feel the positives.

3. Seeing yourself as **unlovable**.

4. Seeing yourself as **unacceptable**.

5. Seeing yourself as **having to do what others want** in order to be "acceptable to them" and then, maybe, acceptable to yourself.

6. Seeing yourself as having to **work harder** and longer to get acceptance and love. You actually get very good at the work but somehow **still don't enjoy** better self-esteem.

7. Not letting yourself **accept compliments** and getting very good at finding reasons to make them unacceptable.

8. Thinking that you **can't make changes** in yourself—that you were just "born this way."

9. Thinking that change is just **too hard**.

10. Feeling or thinking that you **don't deserve to feel different, to feel good**—to enjoy life and to be loved.

11. Letting your **self-worth be dependent on how others treat you**, respond to you, and how you think they see you.

Hopefully, you can use this list of "bad habits" to help evaluate your own habits, to help stimulate thoughts and more awareness of those habits—those physical and mental behaviors that cause you to have a self-esteem you don't entirely want to have!

To help do that, you need to really understand what habits are. You need to appreciate how important they are in your life. I believe our **habits of thinking** are the **main influence over what we do**. They **direct the majority of our feelings and behaviors**.

Stop a minute and think about this! How big a part do you think habits play in your life?

I think we all have thousands of habits that start developing with the earliest awareness. These habits are within us and come forth to greatly influence what we do and how we think and feel. They are very much responsible for our self-esteem—our "impressions of self."

Habit can be defined in several ways.

In Webster's Collegiate Dictionary, habit is described as "(1) a tendency or disposition to act in a certain way, acquired by repetition of such acts; (2) a usual mode of action; a custom or usage, (3) a characteristic trait."

The Catholic Encyclopedia, volume 7, online edition copyrighted 1999 by Kevin Knight, includes a very good discussion of habits and it is not referring to religious clothing. It notes that daily experience shows how the **repetition of action or reactions tends to produce the probability to act or react in the same way**.

As we do things repetitively, they eventually become easier to do, and it takes less conscious awareness to do them. Thus, **habits** are **formed**. These habits can originate and be developed consciously or knowingly, such as when we learned to write. In that process we paid attention to the form of each letter and repeated making it over and over. We were developing a "behavior habit." The more we wrote the letters, the better we got at it. Eventually we formed words, and the writing of letters required less thought—it became more automatic, more of a habit.

It takes effort to develop habits, whether we do so knowingly or unknowingly, and it takes repetition.

I am reminded of one of our cats, Angel, whom we can usually find taking a nap in one particular dining room chair every day at 10 a.m. Angel reminds me how we all are "creatures of habit." She shows the genetic tendency to nap several times in 24 hours and to learn the **habit** of napping, "cat naps," at certain times and in certain, specific places.

In developing habits, a person is often "reacting" to events occurring outside or inside them. We saw this with Mary Ann, who began thinking she was unlovable and unacceptable because she didn't think she got loving and accepting responses from her parents. The more she had those thoughts, the more spontaneously and unconsciously she continued to have negative thoughts about herself. The more a habit is repeated, the more deeply rooted it becomes, and the longer it might take to change it.

Just as we form habits by repetition and energy, we can change them by stopping repetition and not putting energy into them. Acting in the opposite direction and developing a new intentional habit can also change them.

Another way to look at habits is to see them as patterns of behavior made up of three components: (1) willingness, (2) awareness, and (3) practice. In other words, you need **willingness** to learn a new habit, **awareness** of how you are going to learn it or what you are going to do, and then **practice** of the new habit over a period of time. This is discussed more in Chapter 7 and is consolidated into a **learning formula** that I hope will help your understanding. It might also make the learning of new habits or the making of **changes** easier for you.

I don't think I can emphasize enough the importance that **habits** play in your thinking, feeling and behaving. Appreciating their importance in self-esteem is necessary and helpful because **habits can be changed**. They are not something you are born with—**they were learned, and thus you can learn new ones** that will benefit your self-esteem. Since self-esteem is the combination of the impressions you have of yourself, and those impressions primarily result from **habits** of thinking, feeling and behaving, you can get into the driver's seat and determine a new course for yourself—a new direction that you choose. You can teach yourself to have better self-esteem.

I like to think of our habits of thinking, feeling and behaving as our "**habit triads**." We are filled with these "habit triads." I believe we develop a particular thought in response to something in our environment. We then acquire a particular feeling that is hooked to that thought. This thought and feeling result in a specific behavior. This gives us one more "habit triad" that becomes part of our memory bank and adds to the others to influence how we handle life and how we view ourselves, our self-esteem.

Remember, **habit triads** are things **you learned**. Therefore, **you can change them**—you can teach yourself new and better habit triads that will make you more the person you want to be. You can discourage the old, bad habit triads and stop nurturing them so they grow weaker and less influential.

Another way I like to look at "habit triads" is to see them as books on our bookshelf. The bookshelf itself would be like our genetics. It serves as a "framework" for our thoughts, feelings and behaviors and is more "stationary" or unchangeable. The books are like our "habit triads"—we select them and put them on the shelf, and they stay there and influence our thoughts, feelings and behaviors as long as we let them.

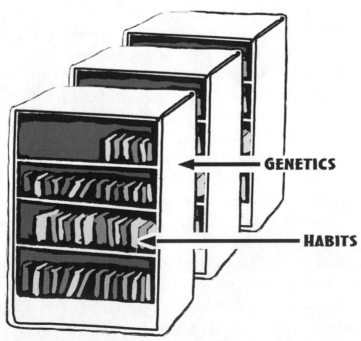

Habit triads, however, **can be changed**!

We can, through **awareness**, decide which ones we want to keep, which ones we want to throw away, and which ones we want to move around or modify in some way.

The question is—how do you begin to make these changes?

How do you move toward better **impressions of self**? Needless to say, the more **aware** you can be of those habit triads you don't like in yourself, the more opportunity and ability you will have to change them.

We will look more at **awareness** in the next chapter.

Pearls:

1. **Habit Triads** make up the main ingredient of our self-esteem.
2. Habit Triads are **learned** as we react to our environment. We react by forming a thought; a feeling then develops and hooks onto that thought; as a final result of this process, a behavior occurs and we have a new **habit triad**.
3. Since habits are learned, we **can teach ourselves better habit triads** and get rid of ones we don't find helpful.
4. We all have many **habit triads** that negatively affect our self-esteem.
5. What really makes us who we are is our "bookcase" that consists of a genetic framework filled with our "habit triads."

Considerations:

1. List two of your habit triads that negatively influence your self-esteem.

2. Can you accept that they were learned, and you weren't genetically "made that way?" What reasons support your answer?

3. Do you see the dominant role that habit triads play in determining self-esteem? What reasons support your answer?

4. Do you understand that all we experience involves our thought, feeling and behavior habits, our habit triads? Write down two experiences you have had and your thought, feeling and behavior habits, your habit triads that go with them.

5. Read more about habits to increase your understanding of the important part they play in our self-esteem. Look on the Internet and check out the reference given in this chapter. Also find other references— write down what they are and what you understand about habits after reading them.

CHAPTER 5

AWARENESS AS BASIS
FOR CHANGE

It can be argued that more than awareness is needed to make change. Such an argument would be justified and true. Many increments or pieces need to fit together to accomplish "change." You will explore more of those in Chapter 7.

Although all the "pieces" are important for the whole process to be completed successfully, I feel the most important one is "awareness."

You have to **be aware of what you want to change** and **aware of what you want the change to be** before you can actually start the process of change.

What do you need to be aware of?

Certainly, as much as possible!

You began the process of awareness in the previous chapters by beginning to look at yourself—at the importance of a positive self-esteem and the influence of habit triads on the self-esteem you have acquired.

To increase your awareness more, you need to "tune-up" your mind and senses. You need to **invest energy in a conscious effort to be more aware** of yourself.

What should you pay attention to?

I think you can combine all the most important items into three main areas: your **thoughts**, your **feelings** and your **behaviors** i.e. your **habit triads**.

These three ingredients are always occurring at the same time and are always a part of you. I believe the thought originates first, as a response to something in our environment, and a feeling and behavior are quickly attached to it, forming a **habit triad**.

Unfortunately, as you grow out of childhood, you often lose awareness of these **ingredients** of yourself.

As you experience hurt, in whatever form, a tendency to avoid hurt naturally occurs. This automatically causes you to defend yourself and to protect yourself, to try to decrease and stop the hurt.

In doing this, you may very likely separate the feeling from the thought and behavior—pushing the feeling into the back of your mind or even down into your subconscious or unconscious.

Likewise, you might separate the thought from the feeling and behavior or the behavior from the feeling and thought. Your mind will take advantage of all these possibilities in an effort to defend itself and stop the hurt and pain.

At times in life, you most likely had experiences that were so strong or influential that to deal with the resulting thoughts, feelings, and behaviors all together was too overwhelming—thus, you needed to "divide and conquer," to limit the hurt, or get rid of the hurt altogether.

This process of separating thoughts, feelings and behaviors becomes another "habit" that occurs spontaneously—without your conscious knowledge. Since we are all "creatures of habit," your tendency is to do what you have done for years—to separate your thoughts, feelings and behaviors without really being aware of it.

That brings us back to the main subject of this chapter, **awareness**. You have to practice being **consciously aware** of your thoughts, feelings and behaviors at any given time or in any situation, be it a pleasant or unpleasant one.

You have to invest energy in making the reconnections between thoughts, feelings and behaviors so your awareness can grow—can be a larger part of your conscious experience.

The more aware you are of yourself, the more control you can have over yourself.

This is an important statement. Consider it one more time. The **more aware you are of yourself, the more control you can have over yourself**.

Let's look at control for a moment. Most people I've seen, who feel a loss of control over themselves and their lives, are extremely uncomfortable. Such a feeling of loss, or diminished control, can contribute to more loss of self-esteem and can even contribute to a person's developing a mental illness.

Control is extremely important!

You can't get control of yourself without **awareness** of what is going on within you, of what is happening with your **thoughts, feelings** and **behaviors**, your **habit triads**.

Getting back to the topic of awareness, there may be a fear of becoming aware. You may feel that it might bring too much discomfort. Perhaps it will.

It is kind of like being aware of a splinter in your finger. Once you have the awareness, you have to decide whether to leave it in or pull it out. If you leave it in, at least you know how it feels, even though it doesn't really feel good. If you pull it out, you know it will hurt more, so you might be hesitant to cause yourself more pain.

You have to look beyond this. What will likely happen if you leave the splinter in, versus pulling it out? Certainly, if you leave it in, it may gradually work its way out. But most probably, it will stay there, will hurt more, and may even become infected. Then it will cause even greater discomfort and more problems.

If you pull the splinter out, you will have pain but it will be brief, and then your body can go ahead and heal itself and be less stressed and able to serve you better.

Yes, awareness can hurt—for a while.

You don't want to see more of yourself for fear that what you see might increase your feelings of hurt—increase your pain.

Perhaps it **does take courage to be willing to look at yourself**—to look into the darkness of your inner self.

Mainly, looking into yourself requires a desire to feel better and to take an active part in the amazing process of life—the process of shaping your life into the form you choose.

You can do it!

You don't have to passively accept the painful habit triads learned in childhood—you don't have to extend those habit triads further into your life.

How would Mary Ann do this?

She would first need to **accept** the basic idea that **awareness** is necessary for self-directed change—that **it is possible** to increase her awareness, and that by doing so she does take the chance of "seeing" things about herself she doesn't like. She also has to be open to seeing and acknowledging the "positive" things about herself.

She would then need to tell herself to pay more attention to her thoughts, feelings and behaviors, her habit triads. Certainly she wouldn't be expected to do that every second of every minute, 24 hours a day, but she should at least have more awareness—to tell herself to especially be "tuned in" to **thoughts, feelings** and

behaviors that are negative and undesirable, as well as those that are positive and feel good.

Mary Ann must practice this **awareness** daily—as much as is reasonably possible. **Awareness** needs to become a new habit; a tool selected by her to help obtain her goal of increased self-esteem.

For instance, when Mary Ann notices a negative feeling, she talks to herself about it—asks herself what thought and behavior go along with the feeling—she wants to be more aware of what it really feels like—decide if it's a habit triad she wants to keep or to change.

Likewise, if she notices a good feeling, she wants to consciously try to be aware of the thought and behavior that go with it. She really wants to **pay attention to what the good feeling feels like in her mind and in the rest of her body so she can recognize it more easily and encourage it.**

I think she would decide she wants more of those kinds of experiences, don't you?

Let's get more specific.

It's evening at Mary Ann's. George is expected home any minute, and she notices that she feels anxious, actually a little afraid. She has noticed uncomfortable feelings like this before but never really thought about them. She automatically separated the feeling from her thought and behavior because the feeling was uncomfortable.

She wants to make changes in herself and has accepted that she must be more aware of what's going on within herself in terms of thoughts, feelings and behaviors; she now pays more attention to her anxious, afraid feelings—to how they actually feel, physically.

She notices her neck is a little tense, she is beginning to feel a headache at the back of her head, and it's moving over the top and into her forehead. She also notices she is a little more "snappy" with the kids. Her stomach feels tense and has increased its "churning." She is definitely aware that she doesn't like these feelings.

She asks herself, "What thoughts and behaviors are going along with these feelings?"

She notices that she has already identified one **behavior**— being more "snappy" at the kids. She also notices that she is going around the house picking up toys from the floor, straightening pillows on the couch, and turning on the right number of lights. Supper is cooked, the table is set, and the kids have been told to be ready for supper and not to run and shout when their father walks through the door.

She then asks herself about her **thoughts**. She has identified her feelings and become aware of her behavior, what thoughts go along with them?

She realizes she is thinking about George—about not knowing what he will be like when he gets home. Will he be sober, and therefore pleasant, or will he have been drinking, and therefore loud, angry, dissatisfied with everything, unpredictable with his behavior, and possibly violent?

She notices she is having thoughts of not wanting to upset him—thus she needs everything and everyone in the home to be just the way George likes it.

She also notices that she wants positive attention from him; that desire contributes to her doing what she thinks would please him. She is aware of a certain sense of responsibility she has for George's feelings and behaviors. This is a beginning awareness of how her self-esteem is dependent on how he treats her; how it is dependent on someone else and not her.

She indeed is getting the idea of how to increase her awareness.

Awareness is the key that opens the door to making necessary changes.

Then comes the process of walking through the door, turning on the light, and either making yourself comfortable with what you find or making the necessary changes so you can be more comfortable in those inner rooms of self—so you can be more comfortable with your **impressions of self**.

This whole process is not always smooth-flowing. You will run into "barriers" as you work with yourself. We will take a look at understanding and dealing with such barriers in Chapter 6.

Pearls:

1. To make a change in self-esteem, we first must have **awareness of self**.

2. Awareness needs to focus on our thoughts, feelings and behaviors, our **habit triads**.

3. Whatever is happening with us, we have thoughts, feelings and behaviors that are all occurring at the same time. Those **habit triads** are always present. With our increasing awareness of our habit triads we can recognize those that are good and those that are bad. Once we accomplish that, we will know which habit triads to change; which ones we just need to modify, and which ones we need to completely let go of, to be the person we want to be and have better self-esteem.

4. We also need to be aware of how we feel physically when we have certain thoughts and feelings. We can learn to "hear what our body is telling us" and to use that as another tool to help us increase awareness of self.

Considerations:

1. Write down the thoughts, feelings and behaviors, the habit triads, that you associate with two different situations in your life.

2. Pay attention to how your body feels and behaves in any given situation as another way to be more aware of yourself. Write down three or more examples of these physical responses that you have had.

3. Write a summary explaining why awareness of thoughts, feelings and behaviors and your body's physical responses are important to building better self-esteem.

CHAPTER 6

BARRIERS TO CHANGE

"Barriers" are those obstacles that get in the way of your reaching a goal. They occur throughout life and can originate inside you or in the environment around you. They make up your resistance to change.

What do you **think** when you face a **barrier?**

How do you **feel** when you face a **barrier?**

How do you **behave** when you face a **barrier?**

Being **aware** of the answers to these questions will help you continue your journey to building positive self-esteem.

Too often, you will see a barrier as an insurmountable obstacle—an obstacle you can't or don't know how to get around. This view leads to thoughts and feelings of helplessness and sadness and increases resistance to change. Such thoughts and feelings are accompanied by the behavior of stopping the journey, giving up, and "no longer trying!"

Needless to say, those thoughts, feelings and behavioral responses to a barrier only continue to encourage and strengthen low self-esteem and low self-confidence.

You don't need that! You don't want that, do you?

To positively approach barriers or obstacles so the result is good impressions of self and good self-esteem, you have to see them differently.

You have to think and feel about them in a different way so your behavioral response will be different—so your response will be more what you desire. Hopefully, you desire positive behavioral responses that can move your impressions of self in a gratifying, comfortable direction.

How do you think you can do that?

How do you think you can perceive barriers in a different way so you won't encourage negative thoughts, feelings and behaviors in yourself?

No doubt, this question has several answers. I hope you come up with some that are different from mine, as that will give you even more options.

What I have concluded about this issue is as follows:

1. See "barriers" as **opportunities**, not **threats**!

   Think about it.

   See how this concept feels to you.

   Does it make any sense to you?

   "Toss" it around in your mind and view it from different angles.

   "Barriers" are **opportunities**, not threats!

   How could a **barrier** be an **opportunity**?

   I think you already know the experience of seeing barriers as threats, and possibly "giving up" or at least getting extremely frustrated and uncomfortable as a result of that view.

   To see **barriers** as **opportunities** could be a real challenge. It is definitely a **good** challenge with many potentially positive results.

Think more about this concept.

Is it practical?

Is it useful?

Keep in mind that **how you think about a barrier determines how you feel about it and how you behave in response to it. It is up to you**!

You **do have control** over this!

As you make your journey on the road of building positive impressions of self, various **barriers** will slow you down or even stop you.

When a barrier occurs, it is an **opportunity** to learn more about yourself.

It is an opportunity to be more aware of yourself. As noted in Chapter 5, that awareness allows you to gain more control over yourself.

With more control of yourself comes a greater sense of security, comfort, and a more fertile soil for nurturing positive impressions of self.

Thus, barriers can really be opportunities and need not be threats.

How you think about a barrier and how you feel about it determines your behavior—your response.

Don't you think that your behavior/response will be more positive—more in your best interest—if you think of barriers as opportunities instead of threats?

Keep playing with that idea until it becomes more comfortable to you.

Toss it around in your mind until it finds a place to settle where it feels good—where it can become a part of your thinking—where it can become a **habit of thinking.**

When seeing barriers as opportunities becomes a habit of thinking, it will occur spontaneously—

automatically—and will lead to a more hopeful feeling, a more positive behavior, and will increase your ability to make the desired changes in your habit triads.

The next chapters will focus on how to make new thoughts, feelings, or behaviors a "habit" or a "learned," spontaneous response.

Getting back to the problem of dealing with barriers, you need to do more than see barriers as opportunities.

Once you've accepted this view and have practiced it, you have to do more.

If the barrier is an opportunity to be more aware of yourself, what then?

What do you do with such an opportunity to really benefit from it?

Again—you are in control—you can choose what to do!

If you are getting into your car and you notice a tire is very low, how do you respond? Is it a "threat?" Do you say, "I'd better not go anywhere because I might have a flat and get stuck?"

Or, is it an "opportunity?" Do you say, "I want to get going on my journey, and I'd better change this tire now so it won't be a problem down the road?"

If you decided, as I hope you would, that this is an opportunity to prevent future problems, even if it's an inconvenience now—what then?

2. Take advantage of the **opportunity of a barrier by understanding it**. Although you can make a change without such understanding, I think making a change is easier if it's understood. If you know how to change a tire—know where the tools are and what has to be done—it's much easier than if you just start pulling and pushing on the tire. Additionally, if you know how you

got the flat tire, you can make a change in behavior, such as where you drive, that could prevent future problems.

How do you acquire such understanding?

Well, one way is to pretend that you are the detective, Sherlock Holmes.

You want to find clues to help you understand and answer questions about the barrier.

"Why is the barrier there?"

"What meaning is connected to it?"

You, so to speak, take out the thought and turn it around and around so you can examine the barrier from different views or angles.

Is the barrier coming from childhood?

Is it coming from decisions about behavior and impressions of self-worth you made and acquired as a child?

If so, are such decisions or impressions still true today—are they still warranted and practical at this point in your life?

Is the barrier even relevant now?

Often the decisions and impressions of our younger years continue to influence and "flavor" how we interpret events internally and externally throughout our life.

Unless you stop and take a look at these impressions—examine them and try to understand them so you can change them, if necessary—they will continue to affect your life in the same way. The way they affect your life may not be what you want. They may be barriers to a happy and more peaceful existence. Thus, exposing and becoming aware of such **barriers** is a **great opportunity** to help yourself be more the person you want to be.

Not only is such an opportunity great, it can be extremely **exciting,** and it definitely helps to view it that way!

In Chapter 4 you looked at and thought about "habits and self-esteem." You saw many concepts, thoughts, and impressions of self that get in the way—are barriers to good impressions of self and positive self-esteem. This brings us to the next consideration in dealing with **barriers**.

3. Focus on the barrier that is more basic or which tends to underlie and support the others. If you have become aware of that barrier, it is important to put on your "Sherlock Holmes hat" and examine it. For example:

    A. The barrier-thought that you are **unworthy of experiencing** "good" or "peace" or feelings of "well-being."

    Ask yourself:

    "Where did this thought come from?"

    "When did it begin?"

    "What happened, or what did I experience that would cause me to believe I don't deserve to have good thoughts, feelings and behaviors?"

    "What have I done that was so bad that I need to sentence myself to a life of unhappiness and unworthiness?" Do I want to continue to think this way?

    Ask yourself such questions and search for the answers.

    B. The **fear of change**—fear of being different from what you are now.

    Ask yourself:

    When did this fear begin? Why did it start?

    "Is this thought, concept or belief one that I really want to keep?"

    "Is it desirable and beneficial for me to hang on to this fear? What will happen if I continue to think, feel, and behave in this way?" "What might happen if I let go of it?"

If the answer is "No, that's not what I want or deserve," then you have to **let yourself** realize that. You have to **tell yourself** that you **don't deserve** or need or want a "life sentence" like that, and that it's okay to make a change. It's okay to let go of that self-defeating thought with its accompanying negative feelings and behaviors.

Granted, the process is easier said than done. It is, however, a process you can engage in successfully.

It is a process that you deserve to engage in!

You deserve to be aware of the barriers that get in the way of your becoming the person you want to be.

You deserve to **understand** those barriers and find the clues to such understanding so you can more easily make the positive adjustments that would contribute to a more positive self-esteem.

You'll read more about the process of making those adjustments in the next chapter.

Remember—**barriers** are **opportunities, not threats.**

There is one more point to understand.

4. Recognize that there is a certain comfort associated with being the way you are—that way is "known," whereas change leads to an "unknown." Change stimulates anxiety and fear, which can be very uncomfortable. The "fear" feels like a "hurt" that has to be dealt with just like the "splinter" example in Chapter 5.

   If you allow yourself to deal with this fear directly—to face it and understand it—you will then be in a good position to decide you don't want or need it. You will be able to see that removing it might cause temporary pain now, but it will allow more comfort and peace afterwards.

   Getting rid of the barriers will allow you to continue your awareness and the **self-directing** of your **thoughts,**

feelings and **behaviors, your habit triads,** so you can be more the person you want to be—more the person you can **feel proud of, comfortable with, and at peace with**.

Thus, when you become aware of barriers getting in the way of your goal, you must stop and examine them.

You must put on your "Sherlock Holmes hat" and do your best detective work to understand all you can about those barriers.

In gaining that awareness and understanding of the barriers, you are then in a position to deal with them—to decide if the concepts represented by the barriers are ones you want to modify or ones you want to entirely get rid of.

How to then make that change will be more completely addressed in the next chapter. Remember to see **barriers not as "debilitating threats" but as challenging, exciting "opportunities!"**

Let's look again at Mary Ann. She became more aware of habits that she didn't like; such as the habit triad where the **thought** was "I have to please George or he will be angry"; the **behavior** of having the house "just so" when George came home; and the **feeling** of fear if she didn't please him, he wouldn't love her and he would become abusive.

She sees the need to put on her Sherlock Holmes hat and do a little more investigating.

Mary Ann thinks about how she felt the need to please her parents when she was growing up. She needed to think that she was "lovable and acceptable" to them, but did not get that impression so she worked harder at trying to please them. Now she's doing the same thing with George. If she pleases him, he will be loving—not drunk, abusive, and rejecting. She wrestles with these ideas and realizes the need to deal with her fear. While she needs to have a certain level of fear regarding his abusive potential, does she really need to have a fear of his rejection? She sees that her fear of rejection relates back to her need to be loved and accepted by her parents, and now by George so she can think and feel good about herself.

She decides to make a change and not let George's emotions and behaviors make such an impact on her.

She realizes that she is responsible for how she thinks and thus, how she feels—that is where she has power. She isn't responsible for George's feelings—how he feels, thinks and behaves is his responsibility, not hers. She has no ability or power to make him not drink—to make him be the kind and considerate person he could be.

Mary Ann works to accept this awareness of responsibility and not let George's behavior affect her so much—not let it stimulate a fear of rejection and low self-esteem that pushes her into doing things she can't feel good about.

As she investigates these ideas with her "Sherlock Holmes hat" on and works to have good thoughts/feelings about herself come from within and not depend on outside sources, such as George, her kids, and her parents, Mary Ann runs into difficulty. She stops to see what is happening, what is getting in the way? She thinks there must be a barrier to having good, comfortable feelings about herself—feelings and thoughts that can generate **positive self-esteem** from **within**.

As she searches to identify this **barrier**, Mary Ann discovers a **thought/belief** that lies deep within her—one, no doubt, that has been there a long time and has been **blocking** her ability to have good thoughts/feelings about herself. She realizes the barrier is the **thought-habit** that she is **not deserving** of really feeling good—**not being good enough** to feel deeply content/satisfied/ happy with herself.

She begins to look at this **barrier** to better understand it so she can get rid of it. When did she start to think she didn't deserve to feel good because she was really a "bad person and not good enough?" How has that **barrier** gotten in the way of positive self-esteem? Why is it there? Does she want to get rid of it? Can she get rid of it? Asking herself all these questions is very frustrating. Sherlock Holmes must have been a very patient, persistent person!

Again, Mary Ann's thoughts go back to childhood. She realizes that all her efforts to please her parents and her impression that there was a lack of a positive, loving acceptance from them caused her to hurt. In a young person's mind, "hurt" results from "punishment," so the natural conclusion is that "I must be bad—I must have done something bad—I'm not really lovable or acceptable. I don't really deserve to feel good. I feel punished, so I must be bad and deserve punishment."

Mary Ann becomes aware of all these thoughts. She also becomes aware of the feeling that goes with them. She feels a deep sadness with them and also a fear of never feeling good—being happy—being content with herself. She can understand that the "behavior" part of this habit triad is the behavior of trying to please others, to do what they want or what she thinks they want.

As she investigates further and thinks more about the barrier habit of thinking of herself as "bad" and undeserving of good feelings and good experiences in life, she realizes that these habits of thinking were based on her parent's behavior. Just because they were mad at each other—just because they were yelling at each other, at her, and at the other kids—this didn't mean she was "bad." Her parents might have been reacting to a bad day at work, or financial pressures, or the free release of emotions and thoughts caused by alcohol. She realizes that just because they were adults and she was a child, this did not make them right and her wrong—them good and her bad.

As she turns this barrier over and over in her mind and sees it from different angles, Mary Ann begins to realize she doesn't have to see herself as "bad, unlovable and unacceptable." She can choose her thoughts. She recognizes the feelings that go with such thoughts are bad, sad, hurtful, fearful feelings.

Mary Ann begins to see and believe that she really isn't "bad." She recognizes the love she has inside—the love for her kids, for the good part of George, and even the love she has for herself. She knows she is a good person; she is considerate of others and now needs to also be considerate of herself. She has identified a significant barrier and now she wants to change it.

There are many more barriers besides the ones mentioned above and the one discovered by Mary Ann. I hope you will use your increased awareness to identify your own barriers and understand them so you can change them more easily.

If you are working hard at this but feel hopeless and think you can't do it and aren't getting anywhere, you need to further evaluate what is going on within you. What kind of **barrier** is this?

You may be dealing with another kind of barrier—the barrier of depression or anxiety. They too need to be recognized and dealt with. Doing so is definitely an opportunity to achieve better feelings and better self-esteem.

Too often, I've seen patients in therapy who were only getting more frustrated and down on themselves because they were not getting anywhere. They were not progressing because the barrier of severe depression needed to be dealt with.

When someone is depressed—with a Major Depression or "chemical" depression—it usually isn't possible to be objective— to see self and opportunities in an open-minded way. One usually feels as if he or she is in a "dark pit." Before progress on self can be made, the depression has to be recognized and treated, sometimes with medication. In so doing, one increases the chances of being raised out of the pit into daylight, where you more easily see where you are and where you need to go and are more able to move in the direction of positive change.

Please review appendix A and B for the diagnostic criteria for Major Depression and Anxiety. If you think they apply to you, schedule an evaluation with your primary care physician, a psychiatric physician or another mental health professional.

Let's get back to making changes in you—what really is the "process" of change? The next chapter will help you with that.

Pearls:

1. As we try to make changes, there is often **resistance** to change that is in the form of a **barrier**: a habit of thinking.

2. We need to teach ourselves to see barriers as **opportunities,** not threats. They present the opportunity to learn more about ourselves—to increase our awareness of self-awareness of our thoughts, feelings and behaviors.

3. Barriers are just **habit triads** of thinking, feeling and behaving that we **learned**; therefore, we can change them—we can teach ourselves something better.

4. We **own** barriers—they don't own us!

5. Recognizing, and investigating barriers like "Sherlock Holmes," can help us understand where they came from, why they are there and if we need to change them.

Considerations:
1. What **barriers** have you run into as you've tried to make changes? Write at least one of those down and note if possible, the thought, feeling and behavior that go with it.
2. Take the barrier you wrote down and investigate it with your "Sherlock Holmes hat" on. When did it originate? Why? How has it influenced you? Does the "investigation" help you decide what to do, such as stop the habit, modify it, or learn a better habit in its place?
3. Can you see that barriers can be **opportunities**, not threats? Give reasons for your answer using the barrier you wrote down.

CHAPTER 7

THE PROCESS OF CHANGE & THE LEARNING FORMULA

If you look again in *Webster's Collegiate Dictionary,* you'll find that the first definition for change is "to make different."

That means a result is expected, and you must take some sort of action to obtain that result. Therefore, you must utilize "energy" in that action.

From the previous chapters, you learned about awareness and the need to identify the good and bad habits you have—habit triads of thoughts, feelings and behaviors.

Now, let's say, you have obtained increased awareness. You have looked into all the closets of your life and on every shelf. You're aware of the towels pushed here and there and some ready to fall out. You're aware that you need to take them out, fold them, and place them back on the shelf neatly, so they stay there and don't fall out when you open the door. You're now aware of at least most of your thoughts, feelings and behaviors and you have ideas about what you want to keep and nurture, what you want to completely let go of, and what you want to change so your habit triads can be neater and less disruptive.

Now what?

Very possibly, you have tried to change before and nothing happened, or not enough happened.

As noted earlier, most people fear change or at least are reluctant to make change—to make things different. I think that resistance to change often results from that fear.

You too might be wrestling with your own resistance. You are afraid of experiencing your "unknown." You might be afraid of experiencing more pain or more discomfort associated with that unknown.

Without change, you at least have a certain comfort in knowing what is happening. You also have a good idea of what will happen as a result of your familiar, although undesirable, old thoughts, feelings and behaviors. In a way, it would be nice if change didn't occur—if you could stop change and have everything stay the same, as long as you're very comfortable with how things are.

On the other hand, that isn't reality—that isn't really how the world and life is.

Change is inevitable! The challenge is to **make change your friend, not your enemy**.

Whether we like it or not, change is happening around us and in us all the time. It is constantly happening.

You don't look the same as you did ten years ago. Most likely, you don't feel exactly the same. Your opinions, likes, and dislikes have probably shifted a little over the years. Most likely, the people and "activities" around you have also changed.

Since change will continue, why not **take advantage of it** by exerting more **control** over what that change will be for you?

Why not invest energy into making the changes **you desire**, instead of experiencing changes influenced by everything and everyone except you? Such an investment in directing your own changes can be an extremely exciting and gratifying experience!

What better investment can you make than helping yourself be more the person you desire to be?

So, how do you begin the process of change?

As noted, you first need awareness, but other necessary ingredients include "motivation" and "desire," or the "will" to make a change. These things actually stimulate the energy needed to successfully meet, and positively benefit from, this challenge.

You need the **desire** to feel better, view yourself more positively, and have more self-confidence.

Although a negative part of self often exists, usually a part of you, although it might be quite deep, still desires love and acceptance and actually believes you **really do deserve that**!

Certainly you can't go back and get the love and acceptance you originally desired in your younger years. You can't be three or five years old again, be held in your mother's arms, and be loved and feel loved. Nor can you comfortably snuggle in the safety of your father's arms and hear reassuring words of acceptance.

It is possible and it is "okay," however, to get love and acceptance as an older child or as a young, middle-aged, or senior adult.

As you begin to see yourself as a more lovable, acceptable adult, you will be better able to comfort and love the child that is still part of you. In doing that, you can help fulfill your earlier desires and needs. You can feel more acceptable and lovable at a deeper level where the impressions of childhood reside.

Thus, when you make positive changes in some of your habit triads and let yourself really feel good about yourself, be pleased with yourself, and have good impressions of self, you will also be properly nurturing yourself at all levels.

You will feel confident and more comfortable.

You will have learned to **generate your own good habit triads,** and not depend on others to manufacture or maintain them for you.

The habit triad of letting your self-esteem depend on someone else is really dangerous.

Do you really want to put your life into someone else's hands? What control do you have when you do that?

This habit triad, in fact, is a good way to give up control and live with a great deal of uncertainty and insecurity. Giving up control will most likely result in greater dislike of yourself—just like what happened to Mary Ann.

So how do you obtain and maintain that control and use it to improve your self-esteem?

You have to **teach yourself** "new habit triads"

You have to understand the **learning process.**

You need to realize that this process is not just an activity to engage in "at this point in time," but it is an activity or process that needs to go on **the rest of your life.**

It's a process through which you can continue to **fine-tune yourself** to be more the person **you** want to be. In so doing, you help yourself stay on life's path in a way that brings you more comfort and satisfaction. It helps **you be in control** of important changes in your life.

Some of the patients I have seen were extremely uncomfortable when they did not feel "in control" of themselves. I'm sure this is a common feeling, and no doubt you can relate to it.

If you don't feel in control of yourself physically and mentally, you become very unsure of yourself and frightened. You don't know what's going to happen or when.

This is especially evident in those who experience panic attacks and other forms of anxiety, deeper depression, and even seizures, heart attacks and strokes.

If self-confidence and self-esteem were not a problem before these events, they certainly could be a problem afterwards. Self-esteem can be severely damaged after repeated episodes of loss of control. Control of self is very important for building and continuing positive, desirable "impressions of self."

To take control of change and keep it, you have to engage in the "learning process." As previously noted, you need to engage in this process **now and throughout your life**.

The learning process begins with your **motivation** and **desire**, which you then combine with **awareness** of your **thoughts, feelings** and **behavior**. You want to be aware of good habit triads as well as bad.

When your awareness picks up a good habit triad, you want to make a really conscious effort to enjoy how it feels.

You need to reinforce the fact that you can have good thoughts, feelings and good behavior.

You want to let yourself **enjoy** these and feel them **deep** down inside.

You want to feel them inside like the warm, comfortable feeling of swallowing hot chocolate on a cold winter's night.

Through the increased, conscious awareness of positive thoughts and feelings, you will nurture and reinforce good habit triads and thus increase the likelihood of their return.

When your awareness picks up any physical or mental behavior/habit that brings you discomfort, you'll want to explore that as well. As was discussed earlier, you'll want to put on your "Sherlock Holmes hat" and find out where that uncomfortable habit triad is coming from and what it's all about. If you decide it's really not needed, wanted or appropriate for this point in your life, you can then "let it go."

Sometime the "letting go" process can be accomplished with that initial awareness and the decision to "let it go." Some people can make decisions to stop a habit and do it right away, but most people usually engage in the "let it go" process over a longer period of time. If you're not in the category that can immediately let it go, you'll have to "learn" to let go of that negative habit triad. To do that, you need to understand and **believe** that you indeed **do not want it** and **do not need it**.

When that undesirable habit triad recurs, as it most likely will, you'll have to talk to yourself again and tell yourself you **don't want it or need it**!

You then have to move your thinking to something else.

Each time your awareness picks it up, you must again tell yourself that you **don't want it** and you **don't need it** and move your thoughts elsewhere.

As you confront that undesirable habit triad in this way and don't invest any more energy in it, it will eventually become weaker and weaker and be less and less intrusive and influential.

On the other hand, if your awareness discovers habit triads that are not entirely desirable and just need a little "fine tuning" or "cleaning up," you can explore ways to accomplish that. You'll decide what you want to change and what you want the change to be.

As the old habit triad emerges, again tell yourself that it's not going to be the old way completely. You consciously tell yourself what the change is going to be and continue to act on that change—to put it into practice—put it into your thoughts.

You may decide you want to teach yourself a completely new habit triad.

For instance, you might decide you don't like entering work every workday and never looking at people and greeting them. When you do that, you get angry with yourself because you're discouraging friendships and interactions that you really want but are afraid to have.

This fear is usually related to a very strong hurt you have felt as a result of rejection. Rejection hurts us the most and "cuts the deepest" so it's what we avoid the most.

You decide it would help your self-esteem to feel acceptance. To feel and get acceptance, you need personal interaction—thus, you make the decision to **learn a new habit triad**. In the process, you also have to discourage the old one.

To incorporate the new habit triad, you have to consciously be aware of what you want to do, such as looking at people, smiling, and greeting them.

Then, you have to invest energy in that change by **repeatedly practicing** the new thought and behavior until it becomes automatic or spontaneous and occurs without a conscious effort. As that happens you will notice the "feeling" part of the new habit triad. You will start to feel more comfortable greeting people and confident thinking, "I can do this."

You may often get frustrated with this and stop the whole process. No doubt you would like to incorporate the new thoughts, feelings or behavior "right away."

It seems most people want results "right away!"

However, it's important to remember that the process of **learning usually takes time**.

Remember when you first learned to read or write?

Most likely, you didn't learn in one day, one week, or even one year. You had to make a conscious effort to identify the letter you were going to write. Then you had to draw that letter over and over. Later, you learned how to connect letters to make words. Then you learned how to pronounce those words and read them. Eventually, a time came when all of that happened spontaneously—when you no longer needed to make a conscious effort to form each letter or pronounce each word.

The process of writing had become "automatic."

You acquired the "habit" of writing by knowing what you wanted to do and doing it over and over—through repetition and practice.

You had learned something new.

Remember:

Learning takes time.

Change takes time.

Another important ingredient needs to be recognized here—"patience."

Patience is the recognition that a process or situation does take "time," and you are "willing" to give it that time.

You may find that "time" and "patience" are the most difficult parts of the "learning process." I think those who give up and fail at change are usually those who have trouble giving themselves the time they really need to accomplish change.

One way to summarize and conceptualize the learning process is in the form of a **Learning Formula:** W + A + P + T = C.

Willingness (to change) + **Awareness** (of thoughts, feelings and behavior i.e. habit triads—of what you want to change and how) + **Practice** (repetition) + **Time** (patience) = **Change** (learning new habits of thinking, feeling and behaving—new habit triads).

Being "willing to" engage in, and being "aware of" the learning process, over time, will lead to change, to new habit triads!

Your having **control** over that process will direct the change where **you** want it to go!

You may need to focus on a few specific areas of change, a few specific habit triads and consider them for yourself. Some possibilities are presented in the following chapters. Hopefully, they will stimulate your awareness of other habit triads you'll want to focus on and exert positive control over by using the learning process and the **Learning Formula:**

Willingness (to change) + **Awareness** (of thoughts, feelings, and behavior so you know what you want to change and how) + **Practice** (repetition) + **Time** (patience) = **Change** (learning new habit triads, that you choose).

This is another **key** to having more control of your life and thus, your happiness—a key to making the changes you want to make so you can feel more confident, calm, and content with your life.

To look at this in a more practical way, let's get back to Mary Ann. Through her acceptance of the importance of willingness— and awareness—she identified a few thoughts, feeling, and behaviors she didn't really like. For instance, as we saw in an earlier chapter, she really did not want to experience all those "negatives" while awaiting George's arrival at night.

She realized she was tired of feeling anxious, fearful, uneasy and physically ill. She put on her Sherlock Holmes hat and realized these feelings were part of a habit triad. The feelings were associated with the thought that she had to please others so they would like her, love her, and accept her so she could then feel good about herself. The behavior that went along with the thought was making the home the way George liked it. As she thought about it, she recognized that what she thought, felt and how she behaved was up to her—the only **power** she had in the situation was over **herself**.

Using the **Learning Formula**, Mary Ann decided to make a change in this habit triad and not let her self-esteem depend on George—to not be afraid—to not be anxious—to not wonder and worry about George's behavior before he got home. She had no control over that—again, her only control was over herself. She had faced the barrier habit triad of thinking of herself as bad and unworthy, had put those thoughts in a more realistic perspective, and was no longer stopped by them. The **Willingness** part of the **Learning Formula** was present, and she was developing the **Awareness** part.

The next challenge was to put her new set of thoughts and feelings into new behavior. She had to begin to do something different. As she thought about making change, she reminded herself to calm down, to slow down. She began an exercise program. She had read that a basic fitness program consists of aerobic exercise for thirty minutes, three days a week, and weight resistance exercise for fifteen minutes, two days a week, so she set up her program like that. She also heard how Yoga was good for the body and mind and how it encouraged relaxation and increased self confidence. She found a small class near the house and started going twice a week. These activities helped decrease her anxiety and helped her feel more in control of herself—she was doing something good for herself and she was letting herself feel good about that.

When Mary Ann found herself worrying and tense about George's arrival, she took a few deep breaths—talked to herself about being in control only of herself and not George—slowed down—calmed down. She reminded herself that she did not want to let George be in charge of her self-esteem. She practiced this over and over. This took time—learning new habits takes time—but she tried hard for the sake of herself and the kids, and she knew she could do it! She had now activated the **Practice** and **Time** parts of the **Learning Formula**.

Mary Ann wants to learn more about herself so she can make healthy changes. She knows that setting into motion the ingredients of the **Learning Formula** will lead to healthy change. The next chapters offer a few **specific habit triads** that we can all consider changing in order to build a more positive self-esteem. Hopefully, they will help you and Mary Ann make healthy changes.

Pearls:

1. **Change** is inevitable—it is happening in us and around us all the time so it's very important that we acknowledge and accept that.

2. The challenge is to make change our **friend**, not our enemy.

3. The process of change and learning is **not new** to us—we have been doing it all our lives—we just have to let ourselves be more aware of that process so we can exert conscious control of it. As soon as we began experiencing our environment we started reacting to it and learning habit triads. Now it's time to be aware of that learning, to take conscious control of it and teach ourselves the kind of habit triads that will help us have better self-esteem.

4. The process of learning and teaching ourselves new habit triads can be summarized in a **Learning Formula: W + A + P + T = C**

   Willingness—to change a specific thought, feeling, and behavior.

   +

   Awareness—of the specific habit triad we want to change and how we will do it.

   +

   Practice—repeating the new habit triad over and over.

   +

Time—like learning to read or write, it takes time for the new habit triad to take root—we must have patience.

=

Change—The new habit of thought, feeling, and behavior—the new habit triad—becomes a spontaneous part of us.

Considerations:

1. Do you believe change has been, and is, continuing within you and around you? Give reasons for your answer.
2. What changes are you aware of in regard to yourself and your environment—list at least three of each.
3. For each of the changes listed, tell if the change occurred because you wanted it to, or because someone else wanted it to or if it wasn't caused by anyone.
4. Do you believe you can take more control over the effect of some of the changes that occur in your life? Do you think it is "healthy" to do so? Give your reasons.
5. Look at the change Mary Ann made regarding her habit triad of allowing her self-esteem to depend on George's behavior and, consequently, feeling anxious and fearful before George got home and behaving like a frantic house keeper. Use the **Learning Formula** to illustrate how she did that and note what constituted her willingness to make change and her awareness of

the specific habit triad to work on. How did she use practice and time to make change?

6. Look at two or more of your own habit triads and see how each ingredient of the **Learning Formula** was used to develop those habits.

CHAPTER 8

LET'S REVIEW

Before looking at a few common, specific habit triads you can consider for change, let me summarize what we have learned so far.

1. In dealing with self-esteem, it is helpful to define it and to understand what the goal is. To me, self-esteem is how we view self in our "mind's eye", as well as how we think and feel about ourselves. The goal is to be willing to teach ourselves "habits" of thinking that will result in positive feelings and behaviors—positive habit triads—which will create better self-esteem. To do this, it is very important for you to think and believe it is "okay" to feel good—**it is okay to give yourself permission to feel good about yourself**. Sometimes we get the impression from our experiences in life that it is not good to put energy into thinking about ourselves. For some people, one area that confuses the acceptability of feeling good about self is their interpretation of religion. You need

to really understand what your religious teachings/ influences are, and what they say about taking good care of yourself. I think you will ultimately find that they are supportive of good self-esteem and can help you in deciding that indeed it is "okay" to pay attention to yourself and take good care of yourself.

2. The impressions we have of ourselves are extremely important. Our self-esteem is rooted deep within us. It's like the "hub" of the wagon wheel. If it is "strong"—if you are confident on the inside—you'll increase your chances of staying on your road of life in a peaceful, secure way. That inner belief system/ self-esteem will influence how you interact with and interpret your environment. It is **important** for **your self-esteem** to depend on what **you think, feel,** and **do, and not** on what **someone else** thinks, feels, or does.

3. Self-esteem development begins early in life. Our early experiences do have an influence on how we perceive our environment and ourselves. Our **thoughts, feelings** and **behaviors depend on genetics plus environment**. However, I think self-esteem depends more on environment and the habit triads we develop **in response to** our environment. Genetics is the "framework" but our response to environment produces the habit triads that "fill in" that framework—like the books in a bookcase. Since those habit triads were learned, they are not permanent and can be changed. This realization is very important and accepting it will allow you to move forward and put energy into making your self-esteem what you want it to be.

4. We all have similarities. One, I believe, is being born with the **basic** and **extremely important need for love** and **acceptance**. If we get that love and acceptance, we develop habits of thoughts, feelings and behaviors—habit triads—that tend to be more positive and encouraging of good self-esteem. If we don't have thoughts of being lovable and acceptable; if we don't have feelings of being loved and accepted, we develop habits to protect ourselves from hurt or habits that we hope will bring us the needed love and acceptance—like the habit triad with the behavior of trying to always please other people. The habit triads we develop can influence us all our life. The process of learning good habit triads and adjusting/eliminating our bad ones needs to be a **lifelong process**.

5. The process of changing our habits starts with a **willingness** to be **aware** of ourselves and our habit triads—both good and bad. **Since our habit triads have been learned, we have the power and ability to make them different**—to change them to the ones we want and like; the ones that can help us lead a more peaceful and enjoyable life. Most of us need to make a very conscious effort to be aware of our thoughts, feelings and behaviors. That's because we learned to separate them as we grew up. This was done to protect ourselves from possible hurt or bad feelings that might occur if we were to continue to be aware of our thoughts, feelings and behaviors all at once. Most likely, we experienced times when we didn't want to be aware of what we felt when we engaged in a certain behavior. This sort of decision and action teaches our minds to separate our thoughts, feelings

and behavior and really be less aware of our entire self. As we grow older, we have to **make** a **conscious effort to be aware of our thoughts, feelings** and **behaviors—our habit triads**. The better we can do that, the more self-awareness we have. The more self-awareness we have, the easier it is to identify which habit triads need encouraging, which need modifying or "fine tuning," and which we need to ignore and get rid of. Such self-awareness is extremely important as it also leads to feelings of having more control over our lives. As you gain self-awareness and start taking charge of your habits, you'll find that you feel greater control over yourself and experience increased security within yourself.

6. As you work with your habit triads, most likely you will run into various obstacles or **barriers**. These barriers make it hard to change habits, and you might be tempted to "give up." Please don't give in to that temptation. **Barriers** are not threats but are really **opportunities** to learn more about ourselves. They are also habit triads that you have learned. All of us run into barrier habit triads. They seem to be a very common part of our life and make life more challenging. To deal with these barriers, I see myself following the example of Sherlock Holmes, looking for clues as to **what** the barrier habit triad is, **when** it came to be part of my life, and **why** it developed in the first place. After gathering all the clues, I can understand the barrier habit triad better. I can see what the thought is, the feeling connected to that thought, and the behavior that results. With barrier habit triads the resulting behavior usually consists of

avoiding something. With this awareness I can then decide what to do with the barrier habit triad. If it's a habit triad I don't want or need, I mentally put a **stop sign** on it or attach a **red flag** to it so when it comes up again I'll know what it is and remember that I've already considered it and decided I don't want it or need it. Thus, I don't have to put any more energy into analyzing it. All I have to do is avoid that habit triad and get my thoughts on something else. I don't want to put more energy into it as that encourages its growth. Sometimes people will run into the barrier triad which includes the feeling of too much anxiety or depression. They might need to get professional help to deal with those symptoms so they can better focus on making changes within themselves. Remember, **change means to make different**. Too often, the word "change" sets off negative thoughts and barriers, causing us to resist, to think we can't do it. Then change becomes more difficult. We need to remember that habit triads have been a part of our life since we started reacting to our environment. It is possible to take control of the habit triads we teach ourselves. When we do that, we give ourselves the opportunity to build a healthy self-esteem.

7. I believe we can make a change—make things different, if we want to—if we have the **willingness**. We can use the process we already know and that we've been using nearly every day of our lives, to make changes in response to our environment. By that I mean, **we are always experiencing and sensing our environment, and then responding to it by learning or adjusting our habit triads**. We use the **learning**

formula without even being aware we're using it. We have an experience, decide on a certain response, and do it over and over until it becomes one of our many habits. What I'm encouraging you to do is to **become more aware** of the learning process—to recognize that I'm not asking you to do anything new, except to have **more awareness,** so you can direct the learning process and adjust your habit triads in a way that will be good for you. Conscious use of the learning process will help you go down your life's path with a sense of greater control, greater self-assurance and more positive impressions of self. This is summarized in the **Learning Formula: Willingness + Awareness + Practice + Time = Change.**

Making things different in a positive way for yourself, can be very exciting and rewarding. I believe this is a great way to invest your energy and that it's definitely okay to make such an investment. In fact, it's **necessary.** I'm not saying you need to become "egotistical" or completely "self-centered." I believe if you really feel good about yourself and have good **impressions of self,** you'll have greater energy, ability and comfort in helping others and in being a positive influence in the lives of others.

Now, let's move on to look at a few "rules" regarding common habit triads that we all have probably engaged in and whose change or "making different" will help us have a more positive self-esteem—more positive **impressions of self.**

CHAPTER 9

RULE 1: DON'T PUT YOURSELF DOWN

In the previous chapters you looked at what self-esteem is and how you can make positive changes in yourself and see barriers as opportunities for greater understanding of self. You saw how you can take control of "change" and use it to learn new habit triads that help you become the person you want to be. Now let's look at a few specific areas where change of habit triads can have a positive effect on how you think, feel and behave—your impression of self—your self-esteem. These changes might become "rules" that you'll want to make for yourself.

How you see yourself, think about yourself, and behave toward yourself today, reinforces and directs those same activities for tomorrow, leading to the same results. It leads to the reinforcement/strengthening of habit triads that you have developed. Think about this. Read it a few times. Do you agree—do you understand?

With every one of your **thoughts, feelings** and **behaviors**, every one of your habit triads, you are having a significant effect on yourself—on your interactions with others and how you live life and what you get out of life.

You are repeating old thoughts, feelings and behaviors—old habit triads—or you're making decisions to go in new directions and allowing yourself to have new experiences so you can learn new habit triads.

Believe it or not, you really are in the "driver's seat!"

Consider the following:

It is okay to see yourself in a positive way!

It is okay to feel good about yourself!

Belief in these two statements is a necessity if one is going to develop and continue to nurture positive impressions of self—positive self-esteem—positive habit triads.

Therefore, if you have a problem with those two thoughts—if you have a barrier to accepting them—you must explore where the barrier habit triad is coming from and what it consists of. You must put on your "Sherlock Holmes hat" and do your detective work (as discussed in Chapter 6) and make the necessary changes so you can allow those statements to be true for you.

Don't ignore your negative habit triads. The awareness of negatives lets you know what you want to let go of and what you only need to "fine-tune."

You also need to be aware of your positive habit triads so you can encourage and reinforce those. Unfortunately, like Mary Ann, you may have grown up learning to be more aware of the negatives. You may have been told or given the impression that your attitude was "bad"—maybe your schoolwork wasn't good enough; perhaps you engaged in school activities and your parents or important others didn't show up to watch. You thought that meant you were really "undeserving" of their attention. You thought you must not be **acceptable** or **good enough** or even **loveable**.

With such experiences, it's very hard not to become sensitized and more keenly aware of **negative** thoughts, feelings and behaviors in yourself and in those around you and develop negative habit triads.

In childhood, you may have seen yourself as the reason for those negative thoughts, feelings and behavior. Unfortunately, that strengthened your negative self-image. From these types of experiences, you began to think and learn that you apparently didn't deserve good thoughts, feelings or behaviors. You became very sensitive to, and aware of events that produced negative thoughts, feelings or behaviors in others and in you. Just like Mary Ann, you evolved into mainly being aware of negatives—thinking negatively, and thus feeling negative.

Sometimes, because it happens over and over again, a negative habit triad gets learned so well that it becomes extreme. You become so sensitive and aware of possible negatives that you "read in" a negative meaning to verbal expressions and/or physical actions of others. This, in turn, influences your behavior around other people. When that happens, others pick up on your negativity and your self put-downs, and they might see this as an "okay" way for them to treat you. They then think they have **permission** to abuse you in one way or another. Needless to say, that abuse can only result in your feeling even worse about yourself.

Mary Ann experienced that kind of negative situation in junior high school. She was shy and tended to stay to herself. Because she felt "not as good" as the others, she made negative comments about herself. She talked about her clothes being secondhand and not nearly as nice as what the other kids wore. Her classmates picked up on her negativity. Since Mary Ann was putting herself down, they felt she had given them permission to put her down as well. They made fun of her clothes and how she dressed; they said she looked "old fashioned" and peculiar. When Mary Ann heard this, she felt hurt. She saw this as further proof that she was unacceptable. This reinforced her habit triad consisting of the thought "I'm not good enough" which produced the feeling of sadness and shame and resulted in the behavior of her putting herself down and isolating self. Her negativity about herself and her "justification" in putting herself down increased, as did her sensitivity to the negatives in her life.

Those negative thoughts and feelings inside you don't really need any help in maintaining their power over you.

They were learned so well that they occur spontaneously and with ease—they are often well-established habit triads.

What needs help are your **positive** thoughts, feelings and behaviors—the positive habit triads. Those really need your **full attention** and **encouragement**. Because of the common tendency towards spontaneous self put-downs and negative thoughts related to self, it is very important to make a change in this area.

Thus, the **first** "**rule**" **of change** in improving self-esteem is: "**Don't Put Yourself Down.**"

Repeat this to yourself several times. How does it sound and how does it feel? Does it apply to you?

You need to teach yourself this rule.

You need to feel it is "okay" **not** to hurt yourself. In fact, hurting yourself is **definitely not** what you want to do.

You need to be aware of the validity and importance of **not putting yourself down**. You need to realize that doing so can severely damage your self-esteem.

You need to accept this as **reasonable** and **allowable.**

You need to **practice** it until it becomes a spontaneous, working concept within you—a new habit triad.

Using the **Learning Formula** to help do this, you need to do two things.

The **first** is to **increase your awareness** of when you are putting yourself down—when you are making any negative-type "fun" of yourself—when you call yourself names that have negative meanings or associations—when you do anything that is a put-down to your physical, mental, or spiritual self.

As you develop increased awareness of your "self put-downs" and **believe** and accept that such behavior is **definitely destructive** to your self-esteem—when you believe you **don't deserve** to be put down and **hurt** and therefore **don't want** to do this to yourself, then you can successfully tackle the **second** step, which is to confront that behavior, that negative habit of thinking.

You'll need to continue to **confront** this negative thought and behavior **over and over (practice)**. Remember the **time** element (patience), and allow yourself **time** to change.

Such repetition is a part of learning a new habit triad—a part of the **Learning Formula.**

It's important to be aware of the need for patience and time so the necessary repetition for learning can occur without your getting frustrated and quitting this **very important** process.

Tell yourself that any time a negative self put-down thought comes to mind, a **red flag** or **stop sign** will go up and say, "Stop—I don't want to do that! I don't want to think that way."

When you find yourself putting yourself down, you have to remind yourself not to do it—you **don't** want to do it—you **don't deserve** to do it and experience the bad feelings and behaviors of that habit triad—it's destructive and only builds up negative feelings, which definitely don't need any help from you. You've already considered the pros and cons of self put-downs, so you don't need to go through all that again; you don't need to analyze it more.

You want to remind yourself—simply, compassionately, and as often as necessary—that you **don't deserve this** and you **don't**

want to put yourself down, and then move your attention to something else.

No doubt, you'll continue to automatically be negative with yourself for a while.

As you persist with your awareness, however, and repetitively reinforce and practice the stopping of "self put-downs," a change will gradually occur.

The old habit triad will lose its tenacity and will be less and less influential. It will become less and less natural and spontaneous within you; instead, it will become a weaker habit. If you stop watering a plant, it will eventually get weaker and die. When you stop repeating a habit triad, it will also become weaker and less intrusive.

As you continuously and repeatedly discourage the "self put-downs," you'll also want to encourage awareness of the "positives" within you and around you.

You'll want to increasingly feel how "okay" it really is **not** to put yourself down.

You'll want to feel how "okay" and **strongly desirable** it is to be **responsible** for yourself and to **direct** the changes you are making—the new habit triad you are teaching yourself.

You'll feel how **exciting** and **wonderful** such an investment of time and energy in yourself really is!

DON'T PUT YOURSELF DOWN!

There is no positive future in "self put-downs" is there?

You really don't deserve to feel worse and to contribute to that process yourself, do you?

If you answer these questions "yes", then you definitely have a stumbling block—a "barrier" you have to look at right away. If you don't look at it, your mind and beliefs won't let you go any further. You have to put on your "Sherlock Holmes hat" again and start investigating that barrier—that bad habit triad. You must ask yourself, "What have I done that is so bad?"

Certainly, you are not perfect and you have done things you aren't proud of, but do you deserve punishment **all your life**?

How much punishment is enough?

At some point, you have to put all this into a healthier perspective.

At some point, you must say, "**Enough is enough!**"

At some point, you need to accept that it is "okay" to feel **good** about yourself.

You have to accept and believe that you've had enough punishment and hurt and it's okay for it to stop. It's okay to replace punishment and hurt with **good** thoughts, feelings and behaviors—with good habit triads.

You need to accept that it's **okay** and **desirable** to let yourself be the **kind**, **loving**, **compassionate**, **assertive** person you want to be.

It's okay to be someone you can feel good about and live comfortably with—someone who can enjoy inner feelings of peace.

DON'T PUT YOURSELF DOWN!

You have the choice to put yourself down or not!

It's extremely important to treat yourself with positive consideration—with respect and love. Most people, I believe, try to treat others that way—why not treat yourself with at least the same consideration?

Again, if you try and it doesn't seem to work, look for what's getting in the way. No doubt, a negative thought and feeling is blocking your effort; a barrier habit triad is there.

You have to pretend you're "Sherlock Holmes" again and find out what that thought is—where it's coming from—what it means.

You then need to ask yourself if it's a valid thought now—is it really what you want at this point in time?

You have a choice—**use it**!

By using your right of choice along with your awareness, practice (repetition) and time (patience), you'll teach yourself to be the kind of person you want to be.

Remember the **Learning Formula**: W + A + P + T = C

Willingness + Awareness + Practice + Time = Change (learning of new habits of thoughts, feelings and behaviors—new habit triads).

You are worth the investment of your time and energy!

You have the right of free choice!

You have the right to feel good about yourself and to make the decisions that guide that process.

DON'T PUT YOURSELF DOWN!

Learning this first "rule" can have an amazing impact on the learning and creation of desirable, positive, self-esteem.

Pearls:
1. A Self put-down is a bad **habit triad** we learned, so it can be changed/stopped by learning not to reinforce the self put-down thought—not to water and feed it. Then we can develop and learn a new, positive habit triad. Remember, **habits** get stronger the **more** we repeat them, but they get weaker the **less** we repeat them.

2. Each self put-down adds more negativity to self-esteem, even when we tell ourselves we are only "joking." The negatives pile up and can outweigh the positives.

3. Self put-downs are often a form of punishment and are definitely a "hurt" to self that we **don't need** to do. They definitely damage self-esteem.

Considerations:

1. List three ways you put yourself down—they might be thoughts, feelings or behaviors.

2. Put on your "Sherlock Holmes hat" and investigate where one of these self put-down habit triads came from and why you do it. Identify the parts of the triad—the thought, the feeling that goes with the thought and the behavior that results from the thought.

3. Decide whether or not you need to continue all your different self put-down habits. If you do need to continue and can't justify stopping, what are you getting out of it? Do you need to punish yourself? What have you done to deserve lifelong punishment?

4. Can you see the value of stopping self-putdowns? Note five reasons.

5. Can you give yourself "permission" to stop putting yourself down? List three reasons to do so and any barriers that make it difficult.

6. Pick out one self-put-down habit triad—be specific. Be convinced you don't need it anymore and list three reasons it's harmful. Fill out and describe the various parts of the **Learning Formula** as it relates to changing this habit triad. Practice putting a "stop sign" on it and ignoring it when it comes up. After that, get your mind on something else. You'll need

to do this over and over, which is the **Practice**. You are teaching yourself a new habit triad—the habit triad with the behavior of **not** putting yourself down. Good for you! Finally, remember the **Time** part of the formula and have patience with yourself.

CHAPTER 10

RULE 2: DON'T COMPARE YOURSELF TO OTHERS
RULE 3: BE FAIR TO YOURSELF
RULE 4: EXERCISE YOUR FREEDOM OF CHOICE

Do you ever compare yourself to someone else?

Do you ever compare your work, financial status, family, girlfriend, boyfriend, kids, grandkids, pets, feelings, behaviors, spouse, or home to those of others? I'm sure the list of possible comparisons could go on forever!

When you feel uncomfortable with yourself—when your "impressions of self" are not positive—I think you are even more likely to compare yourself to others.

More often than not, unfortunately, you come up with the "short end of the stick."

Don't you?

You see yourself as lacking something. In some way, you see yourself "not as good" as the other person.

This negative conclusion is reached because of a couple of factors.

One factor has to do with your "programming" from a young age—from seeing yourself as unworthy, unlovable, and unacceptable. As previously mentioned these perceptions are reinforced over the years and become very strong, spontaneous responses—negative **habit triads**.

In fact, comparing yourself to others just becomes another reinforcement of negative impressions of self, another negative habit. Isn't that correct?

Is that really what you want to do?

You must be **aware** of what you're doing!

These old habit triads just occur spontaneously and usually aren't accompanied by much conscious thought. They've become an automatic response, a habit, because they've been practiced numerous times throughout your life.

It's of utmost importance to be aware and to hook your thoughts back up to your behaviors and feelings. Through awareness of any particular habit triad, you gain more control.

You can decide not to have a certain thought anymore and practice not having it until this becomes the "norm," the "spontaneous thought;" accompanied by a new feeling and behavior. It really is amazing what your mind can do, what you can do—good and bad.

As you develop from childhood and experience more of life, and especially if you experience more of the negative part of life, the mind tries to protect itself from the hurt that it feels.

As previously noted, the mind decides that being aware of negative feelings at the same time that you are having a certain thought and behavior is too uncomfortable. It hurts too much.

As time passes, the mind tends to separate feelings from thoughts and behaviors. Or, it may separate a thought from a feeling and behavior or a behavior from a feeling and thought. The final result, however, is that you end up less aware of yourself— less aware of your own thoughts, feelings, and behaviors, as mentioned in previous chapters.

To correct that and get "back on track," you have to use a lot of **conscious effort**!

You have to use **conscious awareness** so you can reconnect your thoughts, feelings, and behaviors and experience increased awareness of self.

In so doing, you may experience hurt—even pain.

Surprisingly, you may also have good feelings and experiences, which is what you want. Isn't that right?

No matter which occurs you'll be in a much better position to take control of yourself. You'll be in the position needed to direct your thoughts, feelings, and behaviors in the positive, helpful way you really want them to go.

You'll then be able to more clearly see how **comparing** yourself to others is just another **negative** habit.

You'll be able to speak to yourself with true conviction and tell yourself that you don't deserve hurt. You'll be able to tell yourself, and believe that hurting yourself in any way is definitely not what you want to do. **So why do it**?

This then brings you to a second "rule" of self-esteem:

DON'T COMPARE YOURSELF TO OTHER PEOPLE!

Whether you see yourself as better than or worse than others, you need to realize that expending your energy on comparisons is usually not positive or productive.

If you already have a poor self-esteem, or a negative impression of self, comparing yourself to others in any way will usually result in their looking better and your looking worse!

You really don't need that, do you?

Aren't your negative thoughts, feelings, and behaviors strong enough already?

You don't need to help them become stronger. What's the future in that?

Here, again, you need to **accept** and **believe** that such activity is **not worth it**.

You **don't need** to engage in it.

You **don't want** to engage in it!

"Why not?" You might still be asking.

The second factor influencing this kind of behavior is that **it's not fair** to you!

I don't believe you can fairly compare yourself to someone else.

Why? Because you have a broad and deep awareness of yourself—of your inner feelings—your "history." You have a fairly complete picture of yourself inside and out, even though it might be negatively colored and some parts are hidden.

What do you compare that to?

You compare that to what **you see** in others.

The problem with that process is that what you see in others is usually only what they want you to see!

You don't see the full picture of who they are.

There is no way to see the full picture unless you could somehow actually be them. So far, I haven't seen anyone who could do that. Have you?

In illustrating this further, I like to use the analogy of two icebergs looking at each other across the water. As one of the icebergs, you have a full awareness of yourself—the part above the water and the larger part, which is underwater.

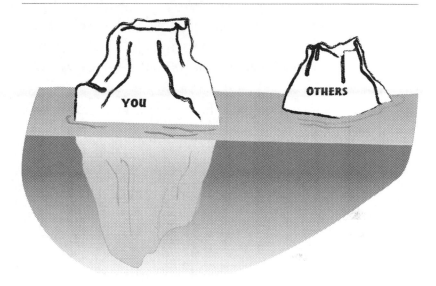

What do you see of the other iceberg as you look across the water?

You only see what's above the surface.

You only see the **smaller part**!

Although you know more is there, you can't see it. All you can do is imagine what's beneath the surface.

As previously noted, how you imagine the part beneath the surface is going to be based on your own thinking—how you see yourself, how you think other people see you, and how you think other people think, feel, and behave.

Is that a good basis for a **fair** comparison?

I don't think so. Do you?

If you really agree, then why do it?

You don't have to!

DON'T COMPARE YOURSELF TO OTHER PEOPLE!
It can't be fairly done!

You at least need to be fair to yourself and with yourself. Even though other people in your life haven't been fair to you, this really doesn't mean you need to treat yourself the same way they have treated you.

There really is no law against this—no law stating you cannot be fair to yourself. There are no laws except the ones **you have written** in your own mind. The habits of thinking you have taught yourself. Since you have taught yourself these laws/rules/habits, you also have the power to **erase** them or **change** them; to teach yourself something else! You have the power to teach yourself a law/rule/habit that is of your choosing and that is good for you.

Have you written an inner "law" against **fairness to self**? A law that says "I don't deserve to be treated fairly."

If so, put on your Sherlock Holmes hat again and explore what that "barrier habit" of thinking is all about.

What meaning has it had and does it have in your life? Where did it come from?

Is it a "law" you really need and want; if so, why?

What good does that "law" do for you? Won't it get in the way of your letting in good thoughts and feelings about yourself?

Sure it will!

Therefore, it's a habit of thought that needs to be changed. You need to let go of it. You don't need it anymore. Really, you don't want it anymore!

That brings you to another rule of self-esteem. You guessed it:

BE FAIR TO YOURSELF!

How can you be fair to others in life if you can't be fair to yourself?

Isn't that "speaking with a forked tongue?"

Isn't that having a "double standard"—one for others and one for you?

Again, I'd ask, is that really what you want? Is that really how you want to be and how you want to see yourself? Do you really want to be treated unfairly?

Remember, **you do have a choice**!

You do have a wonderful and exciting, although sometimes frightening, ability and freedom to make choices for yourself.

Why not take advantage of that?

You really can teach yourself new, helpful thinking-habits; thinking-habits which will create new habit triads that you want! They will be habit triads that will contribute to a more positive, healthy, enjoyable, self-esteem.

Remember the **Learning Formula**: $W + A + P + T = C$

Willingness + Awareness (of thoughts, feelings, behaviors) + Practice (Repetition) + Time (Patience) = Change (New thoughts, feelings, and behaviors; new habit triads).

Remember the **rules** suggested **to help self-esteem**:
1. **DON'T PUT YOURSELF DOWN!**
2. **DON'T COMPARE YOURSELF TO OTHERS!**
3. **BE FAIR TO YOURSELF!**

We can add one more rule from our discussion above:
4. **ALLOW YOURSELF FREEDOM OF CHOICE** and allow yourself to **EXERCISE YOUR FREEDOM OF CHOICE!**

How could Mary Ann benefit from this?

As she thinks about her "laws" of thinking, she begins to realize she has compared herself to others for years. She's seen them as prettier, as smarter, as having better homes and families, and as not being forced to have the responsibilities she has had. She realizes she has made many more comparisons as well and most of them have resulted in her feeling worse about herself. In fact, she doesn't remember any that resulted in good thoughts and feelings about herself.

Of course, she doesn't really know the status of all these factors in other people and in their lives. She begins to realize that how she thinks about and sees others is strongly colored by how she thinks about and sees herself and her life. She automatically thinks others must be better off in multiple ways and that they see her in the same way she sees herself, negatively. Mary Ann begins to realize that she **can't fairly compare herself to others**.

She uses her intellect to see this and to believe that it's okay for her to develop her own positive self-esteem. It is **okay** for her to feel **good about herself.**

Mary Ann realizes there is a part of her that thinks she is good, caring, responsible, considerate, loving, and honest.

She decides that those thoughts need to be **reinforced** by her. She has to be **fair** to herself. Sure, she's made mistakes. Who hasn't?

Those mistakes, however, offer her an opportunity. They offer an **opportunity** to learn more about herself, to make **positive** adjustments and to teach herself positive habit triads just as she decided to do in Chapter 7.

They offer the opportunity to do "fine tuning" using the **Learning Formula (W + A + P + T = C).** In doing that, she can become more the person she really wants to be.

SHE HAS THE CHOICE!

YOU HAVE THE CHOICE!

IT IS POSSIBLE!

IT IS DESIRABLE!

IT IS OKAY!

THERE IS NO RULE AGAINST HAVING GOOD SELF-ESTEEM EXCEPT THE RULE YOU MAKE FOR YOURSELF.

DON'T DO IT!

DON'T PUT YOURSELF DOWN!

DON'T COMPARE YOURSELF TO OTHERS!—There is no **fair way** to compare yourself to others—you could only do this fairly if you could actually be them, and you can't, so why compare?

BE FAIR TO YOURSELF! Fairness is good in all situations.

EXERCISE YOUR FREEDOM OF CHOICE! We have this freedom—it's up to us to use it.

Pearls:

1. Since we cannot be another person, there is no way to really know what that person is thinking and feeling. Other people will show us only what they want us to see—the "tip" of the iceberg.

2. Because we can't be someone else or really know what they are thinking and feeling, there is no way to fairly **compare** ourselves to others, so why do it?

3. Be **fair** to yourself. Comparing yourself to others is not being fair to yourself since you are comparing all of you to only what you see and perceive of them.

4. We have the freedom of choice to decide what we're going to do—what habit triads we'll develop or discard. So why not pick habit triads that will bring good feelings and behaviors—why not exercise our right to **freedom of choice**?

Considerations:

1. List two times that you compared yourself to someone else. List what you saw in yourself and what you saw in them.

2. Do you really think you made a fair comparison? What was the result? Did it help you feel better about yourself?

3. Do you believe such comparisons are fair or helpful? List your reasons for your "yes" or "no" response.

4. Write a few sentences about why it's important to be fair to yourself. List two times when you were unfair to yourself. What were the results? How could you have been fair in each instance?

5. Do you believe you really have **freedom** of choice? Write your response and consider how your response affects your self-esteem and your quality of life.

6. Choose one time when you compared yourself to others. How can you use the Learning Formula to change that habit of comparison? Fill out each part of the Learning Formula so it's useful to you in stopping that "comparison" habit. Do the same for a time when you were unfair to yourself.

CHAPTER 11

RULE 5: INVEST YOUR ENERGY WISELY

Getting anything accomplished even simple mental and physical functioning, takes energy. I know of no way around that. Everything we do—our basic body functions, our breathing, metabolizing our food, thinking and feeling—all require energy.

It is my impression that Einstein's theory regarding energy essentially states that energy really doesn't increase or decrease— it just changes form.

Thus, the energy in a tree is used to help the tree grow and keep it alive. When that tree is cut for fuel the burning wood releases energy in the form of heat. This energy then warms our bodies or warms a room by warming molecules in the air.

Needless to say, energy is a vital, essential resource.

Since you have a limited amount of energy, you need to use it wisely. It's like the fuel that runs your vehicle, warms your home, or provides lighting in your home or workplace. If you waste it, sooner or later you or someone else will suffer. It's important to remember to be a conscientious, thoughtful consumer of energy.

This applies to the energy you pay for and use to run the material things in your life and to your own, very personal physical and mental use of energy.

Either way, you need to remember you have a **limited quantity** of energy, and you need to use it very, very, wisely!

You might ask, how does this apply to self-esteem?

How does this apply to the impressions we have of ourselves?

This leads to another "rule" you need to consider incorporating into your "being." It's another habit that can make it easier for you to build a positive and desirable self-esteem.

DON'T INVEST YOUR ENERGY IN SOMETHING YOU CAN'T DO ANYTHING ABOUT!

Why not?

Because to do so is usually a **waste of energy**!

Again, you want and need all your energy to help yourself be the kind of person you desire to be. Investing it in something that brings a negative return or no return at all is not going to get you where you want to go.

Negative energy investment occurs way too often. A few examples of this have already been brought to your attention. They include:

- The energy you use **putting yourself** down.
- The energy you use **comparing yourself to others**.
- The energy you use in **needless worry**.
- The energy you use maintaining your thoughts of being **unlovable and unacceptable**.
- The energy you use to **hold feelings in and not express them,** and then the energy you use being **mad at yourself** for doing it.
- The energy you use to keep an **emotional wall** in place to keep out hurt.

Unfortunately, another main problem with emotional walls is that they usually keep out the good feelings as well as the bad.

Perhaps this is another area that you need to "fine tune" by increasing awareness of your "wall" and deciding that you can handle your life without it.

Are you maintaining an emotional wall?

If so, question whether or not that is really what you want to do.

I doubt maintaining such a wall is really in your best interest. What do you think?

- Putting energy into **controlling others is also a negative activity** and waste of your good energy.

You really have no significant control over other people. After all, it's usually hard enough to feel continuous control over yourself, isn't it?

The more energy you put into telling others what to do— worrying about what they're doing or might do and worrying about how they feel about you, other people, or other things in life—the more frustrated and negative you'll feel. Most likely, you'll also be more tired and feel drained of energy.

You cannot increase your knowledge and awareness of yourself in a positive way when you are tied up in negative feelings and a negative use of energy!

That doesn't mean that you won't have negative experiences and feelings in life regardless of where you direct your energy. It just means that if you conserve your energy and use it to increase your own awareness and to help yourself become more like the person you want to be, you'll have better results. You'll increase the positive impressions you have of yourself—your self-esteem. I like to envision this concept as having **your own house and your own property.**

You have a **property boundary** around your home. You may or may not have a fence to help you see the boundary but you know it is there. Likewise, your energy has boundaries or limits. Sometimes you might not be aware of where those boundaries/limits are located.

All too frequently, people have problems **knowing where their property ends** and **another person's property begins**— problems knowing where their **personal limits** are regarding many areas of life, such as responsibilities, feelings, desire, energy investment.

If you stay in your own yard and put your energy into keeping your own house and property neat, clean, attractive and comfortable, you will most likely feel good about your home— about your property—about yourself.

On the other hand, if you don't pay attention to your own property and yourself and instead, invest your energy into complaining about your neighbors—telling them what to do and how to do it and worrying about what they think—you'll have a very negative experience. Most likely, you'll soon **feel tired and stressed. You won't feel good about your property—about yourself**—and your neighbor won't be very comfortable either.

You'll find yourself investing your limited energy in an area where you have no control. You can count on this bringing you negative thoughts, negative feelings and possibly more negative behaviors.

This kind of energy investment will result in negative feelings such as sadness, frustration, anger, and even depression and/or anxiety.

It can also stimulate inner feelings of inadequacy and make it harder for you to function in other areas that are very necessary for your existence. It can cause your own, "home"—you—to become "rundown," neglected and "unacceptable."

DON'T INVEST YOUR ENERGY IN SOMETHING YOU CAN'T DO ANYTHING ABOUT!

I realize this is a debatable point.

At times you do invest your energy into other people and other situations, and benefits do occur. This kind of energy investment usually is a good activity and can serve as an "outside" reinforcement of your positive self-esteem—that is, if you let it act as a positive reinforcement!

No doubt, these types of energy investments are selected because of the likelihood, or and at least the hope, of positive results.

For example, you put energy into your relationship with your spouse, close friends, or children. You might be active in volunteer work. When you do these activities, I think you usually expect or hope for positive results of some type-results that bring energy back to you or act as a stimulus for your energy. If such results don't eventually occur, you most likely will stop the activity and put your energy somewhere else.

I realize there are exceptions.

Certainly, there are times when you might invest energy in helping someone else or doing a task for which you don't expect a "reward." You may not receive money or praise or even a "thank you." However, you can still find a personal reward in such activity by your realizing that you've put energy into something that you can feel good about. Thus, it does bring about a positive return to you; it does give you positive thoughts and feelings about yourself—**if you let it**!

Another example of this can be found in Mary Ann's situation. One can see that the energy she invested in her relationship with her husband usually brought her very negative results, such as physical and emotional abuse. In spite of this, she stayed in the relationship and did not leave.

It could be, however, that she saw and felt positive results in the relationship as well. Perhaps she felt positive about having financial security, or about sharing the love for their children, or being needed. Maybe she remembered the love she felt for George when he was sober. To her, those factors were important and helped her rationalize staying in the relationship. **How you look at situations and interpret them determines how you decide to respond and what new habits you will develop.**

Another reason Mary Ann may have decided to stay in the relationship was because she thought she could change her husband and the way he behaved. Unfortunately, investing a lot of energy into "changing" someone else's behavior, especially if they don't want to change, is a fruitless endeavor and a waste of time. Certainly it's a "bad habit." It was important for Mary Ann to understand that trying to change George was not going to be helpful to her. When she realized this and accepted it, she then was able to work on putting her energy into other places where the results could be more favorable. In fact, she then had more energy to work on improving her own self-esteem and giving her kids more of the love and acceptance they needed.

DON'T PUT YOUR ENERGY INTO SOMETHING YOU CAN'T DO ANYTHING ABOUT!

When you do decide to invest your energy outside yourself, be sure to ask yourself if this is a situation where you have a degree of control—where the odds favor a positive result that you can feel good about.

It's amazing how many people have a problem with energy investment. Use yours wisely and efficiently.

DON'T PUT YOUR ENERGY INTO SOMETHING YOU CAN'T DO ANYTHING ABOUT!

Pearls:

1. Each of us has only a limited amount of energy, so we need to use it wisely and efficiently.
2. Using our energy for things that we cannot change is often a waste of energy.
3. We all have limits to what we can do—we need to be aware of our limits and our boundaries. We need to stay in our own "yard" and not use our energy to try and change other people or guess what they might be thinking or what they might be doing.

Considerations:

1. List a couple of places you put energy without having control over the results. Which of those places resulted in good thoughts and feelings and which resulted in bad thoughts and feelings? Do you think you had a choice about how you invested that energy?
2. Do you have **habits** that result in a waste of energy? Which of these do you want to change? Write them down.

3. Are there times when you get into someone else's yard/ activities? Where you forget where your boundaries are in regard to your energy, your thoughts, feelings and behaviors. Write down as many as you can. What is the result of doing that? Do you need to change it? Do you want to change it?

4. Take one of your habits of energy waste and write down how you can change it, by filling out the different parts of the Learning Formula.

CHAPTER 12

RULE 6: THE FEELING GOOD EQUATION

Surely, feeling good is a goal you desire. I think we all do.

You want to feel good—not just for a fleeting moment, but for the majority of the time. In fact, it would be great to feel good all the time. What can you do to help yourself feel better, at least most of the time?

I've pointed out a few circumstances, thoughts, behaviors, and "habits" that get in the way of your feeling good. There are several things you can do to change; and some of them have been previously mentioned. Now you can look at another one. This one has two parts and both are very important.

The two parts are somewhat like an equation, where one side has to equal the other side. Therefore, one side is just as important as the other side.

This particular "feeling good equation" is as follows:

DO THINGS YOU CAN FEEL GOOD ABOUT AND LET YOURSELF FEEL GOOD ABOUT THEM

Repeat that a few times to yourself and see what it feels like.

Does it make sense?

Does it feel good?

Does it seem "do-able"?

How often do you do things that are "good?"

How often do you accomplish goals or activities—large or small?

Learning to **recognize** these accomplishments and to **let** the good feelings **sink in is vital**.

You must **acknowledge** those good feelings and **let** them get into you innermost being. They must get deep down inside. Usually, they must get down to where the child part of you is and where many of the negative thoughts, feelings and behaviors you learned in childhood reside.

It really is okay for you to feel good!

Remember, there is **no law against your feeling good**. That is, there is no law **except the one you make yourself!**

If you've made such a "law," such a "rule," or such a "habit," you can change it and make a new one—a "positive" one.

It's amazing how many people have a problem **letting** themselves feel good!

It would be great if everyone had a loving, nurturing, supportive environment to grow up in—an environment where you learn to think well of yourself and to feel that it's "okay" and "good" to think well of yourself. Unfortunately, you probably didn't have that opportunity—maybe you had only part of that kind of environment, or maybe you didn't have it at all.

In either case, you tried to do what you could to get the love and acceptance you needed. You had to decide for yourself how to go about doing this if you didn't have someone to teach you the right way.

As a child, you may have been taught "feeling-habits" of fear, anger or guilt. All of these contribute to your feeling unworthy, behaving like you are unworthy of anything good and having poor "impressions" of yourself.

Like many people, to get the basic love and acceptance you needed as a child, you had to figure out what to do.

You might have decided that to get love and acceptance, you had to "please" the important people in your life. Most often, these people were your parents.

As you began the process of trying to please others, you learned to "tune in" to what they, and later others, wanted, and you tried to give it to them.

You learned to put your energy into figuring out what would please other people, and that became a habit. You hoped that if you pleased them, they would love and accept you. When they loved you and accepted you, you would have "worth" and "value," and then you would feel good about yourself—or so you thought and hoped!

Some people get extremely good at the habit of trying to please others—and it becomes well established.

Are you one of those?

Do you find yourself trying to please everyone else—or at least those that are important to you?

Do you do this to win their love, their approval, their admiration, and their trust?

How do you feel when you do this?

By now, you've done it for quite a few years. Has it gotten you what you really want?

Has it given you good self-esteem and confidence?

Has it really given you good, comfortable, invigorating "impressions of self?"

If your answer to all or most all, of these questions is not what you're really comfortable with, then it's time for you to make a change. At least part of you is probably aware of this, and has been aware of it, since you are reading this.

Getting good at the **habit** of knowing what others want and trying to give it to them takes a lot of energy—a lot of energy that goes outside you. Your hope is that it will come back in a positive way so you can feel good—so that you'll think it's "okay" to feel good about yourself since other people seem to feel good about you.

Why go to all that trouble? Why take that risk? Why gamble with something as precious as your self-esteem?

Why not use that energy on yourself to build positive "impressions of self"—to develop positive habits that you choose? Why invest so much energy into expecting good feelings from others when you have absolutely no control over them?

That, of course, is definitely what this is all about. Your goal is to feel good about yourself in a very peaceful, nurturing, confident manner.

Your goal, I hope, is to be in control of that process and not to give other people control of it.

The habit of trying to please others in order to obtain love and acceptance is like being on that old treadmill where you go and go and use so much energy and produce a lot of sweat, but in actuality, where does it really get you?

More importantly, where are you going now?

Are you getting closer to that goal of good self-esteem and confidence?

Most likely, you are very competent and have learned to "do" things very well—to put the energy out there and to put the miles on.

So, what is missing?

The other side of the "equation" is missing.

You've learned to **do** things you can feel good about. You've learned to be **productive**, but you haven't put energy into thinking that it's **okay to feel good** about your productivity and your accomplishments, whether large or small, or even to let yourself feel good admiring nature's beauty or taking time to relax.

Now you **can** learn to do this.

You can do it if you're **willing**, if you're **aware,** and if you can accept the benefit of teaching yourself this new habit.

DO THINGS YOU CAN FEEL GOOD ABOUT
AND
LET YOURSELF FEEL GOOD ABOUT THEM

Imagine going to work, working at home, or relaxing and feeling that you've accomplished something good and actually feeling good about that!

It doesn't have to be good in others' eyes, but **only good in your eyes!**

Imagine having a good feeling about an accomplishment or activity—a positive, or maybe "warm," or maybe "happy," or maybe even "content" feeling—and letting that sink in to your inner self. Again, think of letting it sink to your "core," your "nucleus," your "center" of feelings—your "hub."

Imagine how good that would feel and how good it would be for you!

It's like watering and feeding a tree down to its deepest roots. Think of how much stronger the tree would be—how much healthier.

Think of how much healthier your self-esteem would be and how much stronger, content and peaceful you would feel as you repeat this process over and over again.

DO THINGS YOU CAN FEEL GOOD ABOUT
AND
LET YOURSELF FEEL GOOD ABOUT THEM

Since the early habits relating to your need for love and acceptance are usually found in that deeper child part of you, that's where the positive, rewarding, acceptable feelings have to go.

You **can let** it happen!

You **may let** it happen!

You don't have to force yourself—just **let** yourself.

Just open those doors inside—the doors that protectively close off that inner self. Open them up and **let** good feelings and thoughts enter. Then the warm, comfortable light can enter that deeper darkness to take away the hidden fears attached to those negative feelings and thoughts.

Imagine the good feelings going down, down, deep inside, just like you would experience an inviting cup of hot chocolate slowly and smoothly working its way down inside you on a cold winter night. Imagine it traveling inside, bringing warmth and comfort. Let good feelings sink deeply into you in the same way.

You can let yourself feel and enjoy the warmth and comfort that they bring.

You can tell yourself and believe that this is **okay**.

You can tell yourself and believe that this is **good**; "this is what I wanted and what I deserve!"

As you recognize your achievements, as you receive compliments for them or other activities, let those good feelings travel down inside to provide nurture for the positive growth of self-esteem.

DO THINGS YOU CAN FEEL GOOD ABOUT
AND
LET YOURSELF FEEL GOOD ABOUT THEM!

Let's get back to Mary Ann. As you know, she grew up trying to anticipate the needs of her parents, her siblings, and then her husband and children. She learned how to be pleasant, even when feeling sad. She learned how to cook well, clean well, and put unselfish energy into making a home, but she never let herself feel good about what she was doing. She developed the strong thought and behavior—the "habit"—of looking to others for her good feelings—of looking to others for **permission** to have good thoughts and feelings about herself—to have good self-esteem. She learned a "habit triad" that consisted of the thought that she could only feel good about herself if other people approved of her; the behavior of trying to please them so they would approve of her; and the feeling of anxiety and some depression related to figuring out what they wanted and if she could please them. As Mary Ann becomes aware of this strenuous process—this habit triad that mostly results in bad feelings, she becomes more convinced she has to make more changes. She has to do more to have her self-esteem depend on what she thinks and not on what others might be thinking about her.

She decides to open up her self-awareness more and in doing so she realizes she has done a superb job of learning to do things well but never let herself feel, or value the "fruits" of her labor.

She never learned the other side of the "feeling good equation."

Now, however, as she works on building better impressions of self, she wants to feel better. She doesn't want her self-esteem "hooked onto" what other people do or say. She's willing to look at what she does in a different way and to learn "habits" that will build and strengthen her self-esteem.

She sees that there is a part of her that does have positive thoughts and feelings about herself. It has just been overshadowed by the negative thought-habits.

Mary Ann is now willing to give herself **permission to feel good about her own activities** and **thoughts**—to feel good about being a loving, caring person—to feel good about helping her kids and her husband and loving them—to feel good about allowing herself some time to herself, to read, to exercise. She is even considering yoga as another tool to restore her energy and reinforce her connection to self.

She'll now shift her focus away from what other people say and do, and instead, she'll focus on what she says and does; what she feels and thinks. She will redirect energy into herself in a positive way.

Mary Ann will continue to do things she can feel good about and will now open the door of her inner self and **let herself feel good** about these things. When she does this, she'll feel more, stronger, positive feelings about herself, and she'll feel encouraged to continue to use her energy to create her own self-esteem and not depend on others to create it for her.

DO THINGS YOU CAN FEEL GOOD ABOUT
AND
LET YOURSELF FEEL GOOD ABOUT THEM!

Pearls:

1. We can all be the major source of building our own self-esteem if we just **let** ourselves feel good feelings and have good thoughts. It's not a matter of **making** ourselves feel good, but of **letting** ourselves feel good.

2. Most people are doing many good things and have many good thoughts and behaviors. However, they continue on their treadmill of trying to please others. They expend a lot of energy, only to feel frustrated, anxious, depressed and really tired! They have learned to use their energy in many different ways but not to let themselves feel the benefit of what they actually have accomplished. They have learned to do many

things well but they haven't learned to let themselves feel good about that.

3. We tend to make **laws** about many things that apply to ourselves—often such **laws** get in the way of good self-esteem, such as the law of **thinking we don't deserve to feel good**. That is the thought part of a harmful habit triad. The behavior part is not letting ourselves have good feelings; not even recognizing when we could be having good feelings. The feeling part of this triad consists of sadness, anxiety and possibly, guilt. That **law** is a barrier to creating good self-esteem.

4. We need to allow ourselves to understand and to put into practice, the "Feeling Good" Equation: **Do things you can feel good about—and—let yourself feel good about them**. Both sides are equal—both sides are very important.

Considerations:

1. Think about the **good things** you do and list at least three of them.

2. Review how you think and feel about these. Do you **let** yourself feel good about them? Do you let the good feelings "sink in," or do you just make an intellectual acknowledgement that quickly disappears "like water on a duck's back?"

3. Do you run into **laws** within yourself that are barriers to feeling good? If so, identify one or two of them. Do you want to get rid of them? If so, why? If not, why?

4. Pick a habit where you do something good but don't really let yourself feel good about it. What are the parts of that habit triad? The "doing good" is the

behavior part. What are the thought part and the feeling part?

5. Using that same habit example, did you have any good feelings associated with it? If not, why not? Do you need to work on the second part of the feeling good equation? Not letting yourself have the good feelings is a habit. Think about how you can teach yourself to acknowledge and accept the good feelings and thoughts. Try to teach yourself a new habit triad by filling out the parts of the **Learning Formula.**

CHAPTER 13

RULE 7: ACCEPT "POSITIVES" FROM OUTSIDE YOURSELF

Another very important "rule" or "habit" to use in improving your impressions of self is to **LET YOURSELF ACCEPT POSITIVES FROM OUTSIDE YOURSELF!**

As we discussed in the previous chapter, this isn't something you need to look for or depend on for your self-esteem. It can, however, be a nice addition to the various methods you use to help yourself feel better about yourself.

Needless to say, the safest person to depend on for **positive feelings** of self-worth is **you**.

The most important thing is to **let** yourself feel good about what you do and who you are.

Although this is the most important activity, the **willingness** to accept praise, gratitude, and caring from others can also be very useful and important.

Accepting "positives" from outside yourself is like "frosting on the cake."

SELF-ESTEEM CAKE

It's good to have the kind of self-esteem where you don't need praise from others to feel good about yourself, but it sure can be nice to have! It's extremely important that you be the maker of your self-esteem cake but having the frosting from other people can be a very positive addition. One important aspect of this is to **let yourself accept compliments from others**. Then you can get your frosting too!

You need to be **open** to **accepting** such positives and using them to further support you own positive self-impressions.

Many people I have seen acknowledge difficulty in accepting "gifts and compliments" from others. They tend to negate their own value by saying or thinking things like, "If they really knew me they wouldn't say that," or "It's really nothing," or "I know I should have done better."

You can "habitually" deprive yourself of positive input from others and the benefit it can give your self-esteem in many ways. Positive "input" can support and reinforce your good feelings about yourself **if you let it**!

One way to view such positive comments is to actually see them as **gifts**.

COMPLIMENTS

After all, they are something given to you by others.

If they were really in boxes with ribbons tied around them, would you decline to accept them? Would you give them back?

By not accepting a compliment, or "gift," from others, you are actually making a negative statement about their judgment and wisdom. Is that your intent?

This whole process really doesn't have to be complicated or difficult. You just need to "let yourself do it."

LET YOURSELF ACCEPT COMPLIMENTS FROM OTHERS.

LET YOURSELF ACCEPT POSITIVES FROM OUTSIDE YOURSELF.

You need to **let** those positive thoughts, feelings and behaviors sink into your inner self to help nurture and support the growing, strengthening, and positive impressions of self.

Although your goal is to be more self-sufficient in generating the most important thoughts and feelings about yourself, you also need to be open to accepting the many positives from your environment.

You need to **make your own cake**—to be in charge of that process. But if you also get to have **frosting** on the top, which comes from your environment, that's all the better. You can be open and accepting of that.

Don't, however, depend on getting all you need from your environment.

Don't "hold your breath" for those good things to happen to you, but when they do, be open to them—be accepting.

Let yourself acknowledge the positive reinforcements in your environment by seeing them, hearing them, feeling them, and perhaps most importantly, **believing them**. You can then use them to further your own inner growth of positive self-esteem.

That brings to mind how often I've seen people who are mainly tuned into the "negatives" in their environment, as noted earlier.

Wouldn't it be great to use that same energy to tune into the **positives** around you?

No doubt, many of you will say, "There are no positives around me." If that's the case, you have more of a challenge in making a change and **finding** the **positives**.

Perhaps you need to let yourself look at and acknowledge the smaller aspects of life. Perhaps you're looking only for large, more noticeable positive happenings in life to help reinforce your self-esteem.

Is the sun shining today?

Are you warm and comfortable in that?

Do you have a home?

Do you have shelter and food?

Do you have a friend or family, people who care about you?

Are you able to get up in the morning and get dressed, get off to work or school, work around your home, feed your animals, relax? Are you free to worship as you wish?

You may take all these things for "granted," and therefore, you don't acknowledge them as reinforcing positives in your life.

Have you made some **rule** not to acknowledge and accept the more common elements of life as being useful to establishing and reinforcing positive feelings? Do you have a **habit** of not letting yourself see the positive around you?

Here in the West, I often marvel and find a sense of peace in the environment. The mountains change in appearance throughout the day and year. They are full of beauty and have a peaceful grandeur that is reassuring. They are always there; their existence can be counted on. Whether life's events are positive or negative, the mountains survive; they are still there to be enjoyed.

When you let yourself be aware of the **positives** in your environment, you're very fortunate. Positives that come from others, positives that come from the love of your pets, positives that come from your physical environment—these are all areas where you can complement your inner growth of self.

Getting back to our friend, Mary Ann, how would you see her dealing with this issue?

She has to "fight" the old habits of self put-downs and thoughts and feelings of being "unacceptable" and "unlovable." As you may know, that certainly isn't easy. It's an exercise that may not be enjoyable, but the results are definitely enjoyable and make it all worthwhile. Mary Ann is realizing this and is beginning to let herself experience positive feelings that result from **practicing** and **exercising** her **new thoughts, feelings** and **behaviors**; that result from the new habit triads she is teaching herself.

She has never **allowed** herself to accept compliments from others or to really take in, enjoy and benefit from "positives" that come from outside herself. How could she do that when she felt that she was "unacceptable and unlovable," and "looking outside" usually brought in hurt feelings?

However, Mary Ann now realizes her **right** to feel good. She recognizes her self-imposed rules and habits against feeling good and having positive impressions of self, and she's more open to **practicing** the **new** and **positive thoughts and behaviors**. These will in turn result in new habit triads that will bring her a greater sense of comfort and peace.

Mary Ann has frequently received compliments on how attractive she looks, and how responsible, sensible, and intelligent she is, but she has never allowed these "gifts" of positive energy and thoughts to sink in and strengthen and nourish her inner self—her "hub." As you saw in Chapter 2, many thoughts and habits can be barriers that keep such positives out.

Mary Ann now is beginning to **let** those compliments be a source of additional reinforcement to her self-esteem.

She is also noticing other positives in her environment—the beautiful sunsets, the freshness following a summer rain, and the simple joy and love in her children's smiles and hugs. She sees that there really are "enhancing" thoughts, feelings, behaviors, events, objects, and experiences in her environment.

She is **allowing** herself to absorb the positive thoughts, and feelings from them and is beginning to see and feel how much that helps, not only her, but also her family and her whole life.

Although these "outside" factors are not the "cake," they really do make a great "frosting," and it's okay to have that too. While it's not good to depend on the frosting or to "hold your breath" for it, it is okay, and in fact, wonderful to allow yourself to accept the positive outside factors and use them to help create and reinforce your positive impressions of self. Mary Ann has taught herself a new habit triad where the thought is thinking that it is ok to let positives from the environment in; the behavior is actually letting those positives in; and the feeling is usually one of satisfaction and feeling good about self.

Remember:

**LET YOURSELF ACCEPT COMPLIMENTS FROM OTHERS.
LET YOURSELF ACCEPT POSITIVES FROM OUTSIDE
YOURSELF.**

You can learn these positive habit triads for good self-esteem by using the **Learning Formula** (W + A + P +T = C)
You deserve to feel good!

Pearls:

1. We need to be the main source of the good thoughts and feelings that build our positive self-esteem. **We need to be the maker of our own self-esteem cake.**

2. Relying on the words and behaviors of others to be the source of our good self-esteem is dangerous since we have no control over others. Would you rely on someone else to feed you or dress you if you were capable of doing so yourself?

3. The good we can receive from our environment—from people, nature, and other animals—needs to be a minor consideration as we build positive self-esteem, but it's still an **important consideration** and we need to pay attention to it; to acknowledge it and use it in a good way.

4. It's important to accept the benefits of positive things around us that will complement our good self-esteem and help make it stronger. Having frosting on our cake is okay and even makes it better.

<u>Considerations</u>:

1. What people, animals, and natural phenomena can you identify in your environment that can be reassuring and positive additions to building self-esteem? List at least three and explain how each one helps or can help you feel better.

2. Are you **letting** these environmental factors help you build positive self-esteem? If not, what's getting in the way? Are you making the cake or just looking for frosting? Are you **accepting** frosting on your cake when it's offered or available? Write down your response to these questions.

3. Write down a situation when you've not accepted a compliment and, using the **Learning Formula**, show how you can develop the habit of allowing yourself to accept **positives** from outside yourself. What will the new habit triad be as a result. The behavior part will be letting yourself acknowledge and use the environment positively. What do you think the thought part and feeling part would be?

CHAPTER 14

STAYING ON THE ROAD OF LIFE

As many of you know, staying on your own road of life is another endeavor that is definitely more easily said than done!

Your intentions are usually good, but somehow you don't follow through.

You intend to make changes, but life gets in the way—your inner life and the life all around you.

One acknowledgement you need to make is the acceptance of **change**, as previously noted in Chapter 6.

You have to accept that **change is inevitable**. It is always occurring and will continue to occur. Your body changes as you get older. Your perspective, likes and dislikes undergo change. The things around you change.

Most of the time, the changes that have an effect on you occur without your conscious guidance or control. This applies whether the changes are internal or external.

It's hard to keep your balance with all these changes going on.

It's easy to "fall off the path of life" that you were determined to stay on.

So what do you do about this?

How do you stay on **course**?

Again, you have to activate your "willingness" and "awareness." You have to be **willing to invest energy in yourself**.

Looking back at Mary Ann, we see that, unfortunately, she met nearly every day with thoughts that it could be no better than the former day. She initially saw her treatment of others and how she was treated as unchangeable. She saw herself as undeserving of good feelings. She saw herself as unworthy of love and acceptance by others. She never really thought it could be different—because it never had been. She looked to others for positive reactions she could use to feel temporary good self-esteem.

Mary Ann's parents fought, physically and verbally, for years. She was doing good just to get from one day to the next with minimal feelings of hurt and pain. These were the harsh realities she had to deal with. She didn't have time to even consider the possibility of feeling happy, peaceful or good about herself—such expectations were lost years ago. Her perception of self was formed by how she experienced life—what she saw, heard, and felt. Your own perceptions are influenced every moment in the same way.

What you **do** with this "influence" is really **up to you**.

Since it takes energy to deal with this influence and you only have a certain amount of energy in you, it's extremely important to use your energy wisely.

Why not use that energy to **develop, reinforce**, and/or fine tune **positive, peaceful** thoughts and feelings—positive habit triads?

There really is no law or rule against your feeling good, is there?

Of course, as previously noted, you may have made your own laws—laws that say you "don't deserve" or "can't" or "won't" feel good about yourself.

However, no external "law" like that exists. Mary Ann must have had similar inner laws or rules that controlled her and helped keep her in a very negative spot in regard to her thoughts, feelings and behaviors—until she became more aware and willing to change.

I know it can be very difficult to understand and believe that how you see yourself involves a great deal of **choice** on your part.

Sure, the past is influential and often unfair.

Sure, a lot has happened to you and around you that didn't feel good and over which you had no control.

Now, however, that can be different. You are older. As a result, your thinking and perceptual abilities are more broad and objective.

You **do have more choices** and a **better ability** to make those choices.

The bottom line is—**you have the basic responsibility for yourself!**

As the saying goes, "The buck stops here."

You know yourself the best. After all, you're with yourself 24 hours a day and 365 days a year.

Now you have a great deal of responsibility for how you think, how you feel, and how you behave—responsibility for the "habits triads" you want to continue, the ones you want to change, and the new ones you want to learn.

If you can **accept** that concept—that **responsibility**—you can start on your path to a new and/or greater sense of freedom, hope, and peace.

What a wonderful feeling that would be—what a wonderful, exciting experience to feel hope—to experience inner peace!

Mary Ann was able to "step back" and let the "adult" part of her objectively view her thoughts, feelings and behaviors. She saw that she was giving in to her husband's negative behavior, and in so doing, she was telling him that it was okay for him to treat her abusively.

She let herself become more aware of herself, and she realized she didn't like being treated that way. She even came in touch with a small part of herself that knew she didn't deserve to be treated that way. She found thoughts inside telling her that she did want to feel good about herself and wanted to have positive relationships. With this awareness, she was then in a better position to see that she was making choices that were continuing her negative life experiences and negative self-concept. She was in a better position to see that she had the **option**, the very important option, of **choice** and **change** that would help her get on, and stay on, a more desirable road of life.

You have to be **willing** to accept the **inevitability** of **change**.

You have to be **willing** to be **aware** of your **thoughts**, **feelings** and **behaviors—aware of yourself—your "habits triads."**

In so doing, you will know yourself better.

The better you know yourself, the more self awareness you'll have, and you'll have an increased ability to see where you are and where you're going. You'll also have a better idea about certain aspects of yourself—the habits triads you want to **reinforce**, **change**, or completely **let go**.

With such knowledge, you can then "fine-tune" and "guide" yourself to be more like the person you want to be. In so doing, you're helping yourself stay on the path of life that **you have chosen**, not some path of life that you've been pushed onto or off of by other forces in life.

Oftentimes, **awareness of self** has to be learned.

If you grew up in a loving, accepting environment that encouraged self-awareness, you are very fortunate. Most likely, that's not entirely the case, and you need to help yourself by increasing awareness of your **thoughts, feelings** and **behaviors,** of your habit triads.

You need to learn how to see the positives in yourself so you can then reinforce them and build **positive, healthy impressions of self**.

Such awareness of self will then help you see what you like about yourself and, therefore, want to **reinforce** and encourage.

It will help you see what aspects of yourself you don't like and want to **discourage** or **modify**.

It will help you see what new behaviors or habits you want to **learn** so that, all in all, you can be more like the person you want to be.

When you're aware of yourself in these ways and are using that awareness to become the person you want to be, to learn habit triads you decide are good for you, you are then creating and directing the path of life that you desire.

Since change is inevitable in one way or another, why not influence it as much as you can? Why not direct that change so it's good for you and helps you to become the person that you want to be?

The area where you have the power to influence change is within yourself. The only person you can change is you.

To initiate and maintain such change, you need **willingness** and **awareness**.

You need an idea of how you want to be.

You need to accept that change is occurring and will continue to occur, so you might as well exert your influence on it now and continue that influence for the rest of your life.

You need to know how to reinforce desirable habits, discourage negative ones, and make changes. You don't have to make a lot of changes to influence your self-esteem. Keep in mind what happens when you, or someone else, are driving and you turn the steering wheel a tiny bit. As you move down a straight road your direction changes more and more the further you go and before you know it, the seemingly little change becomes a big one. The same thing happens as you take control of building your self-esteem. You make a seemingly small change in a habit or two now, but it results in a big change as you move further down your road of life and because you continue to be aware of yourself and do the fine-tuning of habits, you actually create a road of life you can stay on and feel good about.

You need to remember the learning formula (W + A + P + T = C). WILLINGNESS + AWARENESS + PRACTICE (repetition) + TIME (patience) = CHANGE (new habits of thoughts, feelings or behaviors—new habit triads).

With the use of the Learning Formula becoming an active part of your life, you'll have more input regarding the path you take in life and more ability to stay on that path. It will make it easier for you to teach yourself positive habit triads that you have chosen. Then you can more confidently move down the Road of Life you choose.

Pearls:
1. **Change is inevitable.** It's happening all the time—in us and around us.
2. We need to have direction in life—a path **we** want to go down. It's okay if we change that path as life goes on. Most likely it's going to change anyway. It's just very important that it is **our** path and to remember—the **greatest power we have to make change is making change in ourselves; in our habit triads.**

3. Our major responsibility is for our own thoughts, feelings and behavior, our own habit triads.

4. Through self-awareness, we can work with ourselves and put energy into adjusting our habit triads so we can stay on the path of life **we choose**. I think we are often afraid and discouraged to make changes because we think we have to change our whole self or all of our bad habits. That really isn't the case. Again, just one or two habit triad changes will make a tremendous difference as we move down our path of life.

Considerations:

1. Take a look at the **changes** you have seen that have had an effect on you; changes **within** yourself and changes **outside** yourself. List two of each.

2. Can you accept/believe that change continues to occur, and that it's important for you to be more in control of the changes in your habit triads; the changes inside you? Write down what value you see in that. Are there any barriers you need to deal with? If so, what are they? How can you deal with them?

3. What is your present **path** in life? What do you want to be, do and feel now and in the future? List at least two positive things about yourself—things that relate to thoughts, feelings and behavior. Do you reinforce those in yourself? Do you let yourself feel good about those attributes? Can they continue to help you on your road in life?

4. List at least two thoughts, feelings or behaviors that are getting in the way of your journey. How can you change them? Write down your response. Take one of them and show how you can change that into a positive habit triad, using the Learning Formula.

CHAPTER 15

PEACE

Wouldn't it be great if **you** felt "inner and outer peace" at least most of the time?

Wouldn't it be great if **everyone** in the world recognized, respected and sought the merits of peace?

Wouldn't it be great if each of us did our part to handle anger in a constructive manner instead of a violent, or even a non-violent, destructive manner?

Wouldn't it be great if such a respect for peace extended among individuals as well as groups of people—among nations?

Such a picture is hard to imagine, yet the idea of **pervasive peace** is **very desirable**.

Maybe if you could imagine such a picture—if you could visualize it or at least **visualize peace** within yourself, it might actually be possible to get there. At least it might be possible to get a lot closer to it than you are now.

You might say "I don't have the power to change national attitudes and behaviors," and I would agree with you.

What **do you** have the power to influence—to change?

You can influence and change yourself!

Just think what it would be like if all of us did this in a positive, healthy way and encouraged others in their efforts to do the same!

Mary Ann always wanted to have such an inner feeling of peace, but she never thought she could achieve it or that she even deserved it!

As she realized the **power** of choice she had in her own life, as well as her limited **energy**, Mary Ann wanted to use those precious personal resources to develop positive "impressions of self"—to develop positive **habit triads**. She began to realize that having such **peace** is possible. In fact, as she exercised her willingness and awareness, used them to practice new habits of thinking, feeling, and behaving and gave them the time to "take hold," she **began to feel better** about herself.

She didn't rely on others for her good thoughts and feelings but learned to be the primary source of her own positive self-esteem. She learned to make a really good self-esteem **cake**.

Because of the traumas and heartaches of her life, Mary Ann always had inner spiritual thoughts and feelings of a **higher power**, a God or some force or something much stronger then she, who loved her and accepted her "no matter what." At times, the strength of that belief varied. In fact, at times she even doubted its existence.

As she allowed herself to invest positive energy in herself and learned not to put herself down, compare herself to others, or engage in other habit-behaviors that have a negative effect on self-esteem, Mary Ann actually experienced a **freeing** of her spiritual self.

She noticed that she also allowed herself to connect with the **positives** inside and outside herself. There was more beauty and awe in the environment around her. The sky was bluer, the clouds more white, the breeze was more refreshing, and the sounds of nature were more pleasant and re-assuring. She could see the goodness inside herself—her love of people, her willingness to help others. She could also see the love she had for herself and the need to take good care of self and nurture good self-esteem so she could maintain positive energy to help people and things outside herself. She felt a growth and strengthening of her faith in a superior presence that was giving her support and strength.

With this newfound spiritual growth and confidence, Mary Ann began to experience feelings of **inner peace**. This then spread into her behaviors, which were more adult—more objective and assertive but still sensitive and caring to herself and to others.

As Mary Ann continued to use the **Learning Formula** to positively strengthen her impression of self and learn positive habit triads, she saw that the process didn't take as much conscious effort as when she began. It started to become more **automatic**—more spontaneous, more of a habit. Awareness of how automatic it became gave her a feeling of progress and accomplishment, which she was then willing to accept and to feel good about. These new habit triads created a personal environment where she could feel secure and more calm, peaceful and confident—more in control of herself.

Such an inner environment also influenced her thoughts, feelings, and behaviors in a positive way that was noticeable to her children and husband. They saw her as calmer, more genuinely pleasant, and more willing to be assertive—to express herself, her thoughts, and feelings without fear of their responses, but also with an appreciation of their right to respond.

These changes in Mary Ann's **habits** of **thoughts**, **feelings**, and **behaviors**, stimulated her children and husband to be more aware of their own habits triads. The changes also positively impacted their respect for Mary Ann and the way they treated her—the way they interacted with her. Like a pebble dropped into a pond causing ripples that go out and touch surrounding areas, Mary Ann's new, positive habit triads influenced her family in a positive way.

She became more confrontational with George about how drinking negatively affected his personality—his behaviors—and how she thought, felt and behaved when that happened.

Mary Ann decided to first tell George, when he was clear headed and sober, how she felt when he came home intoxicated. She shared how those feelings affected her behavior and how they even influenced the children—how they felt fear, anxiety, and uncertainty.

She also told him she was going to make a change in herself. She knew it wouldn't be easy and it would take time, but it was an important and necessary thing to do. She hoped he would change, too, and not continue his alcohol dependence. She let him know she loved him—loved the sober him.

She told George and herself that she would not rush around trying to make everything the way she thought he wanted it—that she would do the cooking as usual unless there was another activity that was more important at that time—that she certainly didn't intend to let the house be a perpetual mess, but that she was willing to accept a little more mess than usual in exchange for a little peace of mind and not frantically feeling compelled to do something every minute to keep him from being angry.

She also let George know that if he couldn't control himself—be non-violent and non-threatening—she would have to consider other options such as calling the police and having him leave—or she and the kids might leave.

This was a lot to think about and involved big changes and **"chance taking"** for Mary Ann.

With that information, George might see that he is in danger of losing that which he really appreciates and loves most in life—his family. As a result, he might begin to realize that he can't get away with such behavior—can't continue to be abusive to Mary Ann and his children and retain their respect, support, and maybe even their presence. Hopefully, George will see that excessive drinking of alcohol is a brief pleasure or an escape from his discomforts, but all in all, it just adds to his problems. Drinking actually threatens his having the kind of life he really wants—both his internal life and external life.

Through Mary Ann's example, George began to think about his own awareness and to struggle with his willingness to make changes in himself. George began to see that it really might be possible to have good feelings and thoughts; to obtain a sense of inner calm, confidence, and peace; and to be in control of developing these areas of his life. He could be in control of nurturing himself in a way that would help him have the kind of inner life he really wants. Such an accomplishment would, in turn, benefit his "outer life."

Mary Ann continues to move in a direction she can, and does, feel good about. She is experiencing more peace within herself. She is becoming a better example for George and their children. Her positive changes in her self-esteem are an example for them and shows them that a person doesn't have to stay the same. They can make changes that help their self-esteem and self-confidence. They can teach themselves new and more positive habit triads.

If you and I put our energy into creating and reinforcing a **positive**, **healthy**, self-esteem—positive, healthy **impressions of self** and **positive habits triads**, this would open the door to inner peace. A more peaceful, fulfilling life would be possible!

As I have talked with many patients and become more aware of myself, I am reminded more and more of the widespread desire for a sense of **peace** within all of us.

This sense of peace may be defined in different ways. I define it as an "inner calmness" associated with contentment and satisfaction with self—an **inner environment** where you are confident of and comfortable with, your thoughts, feelings, and behaviors.

Where you feel **control** over yourself.

Where having good self-esteem is **okay** and desirable.

Where **change** is not a **threat**, but an **opportunity**.

Where you are aware of, and in **control** of, your negative habits, your barriers, and your thoughts, feelings, and behaviors so you can minimize any negative influence and make positive changes.

Where you are **aware of your ability and your desire** to fine-tune yourself to continue to be more the **person you want to be**.

Where you automatically incorporate the **Learning Formula**—the equation of **Willingness + Awareness + Practice + Time = Change**—new positive habit triads thoughts, feelings and behaviors.

Where **change is your friend**, not your enemy.

Where you have taught yourself not to do those things that cause negative self-esteem—**not to put yourself down**, **not to compare yourself** to other people, **not to invest energy into something you can't do anything about**.

Where you **do things you can feel good** about and **let yourself feel good** about them.

Where you recognize and utilize your **freedom of choice** to help you achieve positive changes that build **healthier impressions of self-healthier** habit triads.

Where you are **fair to yourself** as well as others and accept the positives in the environment that can help provide frosting to your self-esteem cake.

Where **you** are **active** in keeping yourself on **your** desired path in life.

Where your thoughts, feelings and behaviors are more **comfortable**.

Where the stage is then set for the occurrence of **positive inner growth and inner peace.**

I feel that a very important **companion** to this whole process is **your spiritual self**.

Many would argue that this is the most important aspect of you, while others would say it's not important, or that it doesn't even exist. **The existence and/or acknowledgement of that part of yourself is your choice.**

Through my experiences as a physician—a psychiatrist—I have found the vast majority of my patients do believe in the existence of a **Higher Power**.

You may or may not gain more support and "strength" from that belief than others.

On the other hand, it might be an area in which you need to explore your thoughts, feelings and behaviors and decide what path you want to follow.

It reminds me of the Alcoholics Anonymous program. I believe it has, overall, been the most productive program for obtaining and maintaining sobriety for many different types of habits. A cornerstone of the program is the belief in a **Higher Power**. This is supported by a study on grieving entitled, "The Course of Normal Grief," by Stephen R. Schuchter, M.D., and Sidney Zisook, M.D. This study noted the importance of faith in the course of dealing with normal grief. For two, seven and 13 months after the death of a spouse, most of those in the study felt that "there is an important reason why everything happens." Also, 70 percent of the controls (the other group in the study) felt the same. Likewise, at two, seven, and 13 months after death of a spouse, the majority of surviving spouses felt that "prayer has helped me with my feelings." The majority, from 67 to 71 percent, also felt that "there is great meaning in my religion."

Some people can't or won't relate to or use AA because they can't or won't accept the viewpoint of the existence of such a **Power**. That too, is a choice and alternative programs have been developed.

I believe that **acceptance of a Higher Power, of a spiritual belief system, is very helpful to self-esteem**. I find this is true as long as the spiritual beliefs are positive and not focused on human power, such as in a dictatorship, or on some other negative power, but indeed on a higher spiritual force beyond our total comprehension—a force that can be a positive, loving, strengthening influence on our **impressions of self**.

Within such a spiritual framework, you can find a rich environment to nurture your acceptance of self—a rich environment in which you can positively shape yourself.

It's an environment in which you can experience growth of positive self-esteem.

You might think your whole self having to do with thoughts, feelings and behavior is your spiritual self. Or you might think that the spiritual part of yourself is a portion or piece of the "mosaic" that makes up your thoughts, feelings and behavior.

Needless to say, there is no way to give adequate exposure to this topic in a few pages. Personally, I think it is an extremely important part of our being.

Spirituality can be a very important element having to do with self-esteem.

It can be like the **mortar** that holds the bricks of our self-esteem together.

It's a force that can give us energy and hope—the **template** for positive feelings about self.

It can be that which makes **peace** possible.

Earlier, you looked at your basic need for **love and acceptance** and how that need shapes your thoughts, your feelings, and your behaviors in regard to yourself and others—how that need influences your inner and outer worlds by causing the formation of multiple habit triads.

Why even look for love and acceptance?

Why are they such a driving force in you?

Perhaps it's because they provide a basis—a framework—a **fertile soil** for the growth of **inner peace**!

You can accomplish such positive thoughts, feelings and behaviors and **find peace**.

You can allow yourself to use the **Learning Formula** of **willingness** + **awareness** (of thoughts, feelings and behaviors) + **practice** (repetition) + **time** (patience) to achieve **change** (new habit triads that are the ones **you** desire).

You, too, can benefit from the **positive** investment of energy in yourself. You can begin to experience the **confidence** of positive self-esteem, the **contentment** of spiritual growth, and the **realization** of inner peace that grows in the **hub** of your being and is controlled by you. It is the **heart** that is the **wellspring of life—your life.**

It is a **peace** that comes with **positive impressions of self.**

A **peace** that fills you with warmth on a cold day and coolness on a hot day.

If your inside self is at peace, there will be less hurt.

If your inside self is at peace, there will be less pain.

Perhaps that is the goal!

Then, indeed, your **heart** will be the **wellspring of the life** you desire—that you deserve.

Have a wonderful self-esteem journey. Remember, it's **your journey**—no one else's.

APPENDIX A: MOOD DISORDERS

According to the <u>American Psychiatric Association's Diagnostic and Statistical Manual of Mental Disorders IV (DSM IV-TR)</u>, mood disorders consist of the following diagnostic categories:

Depressive Disorders:
Major Depressive Disorder
Dysthymic Disorder
Depressive Disorder, NOS
Bipolar Disorders:
Bipolar I Disorder
Bipolar II Disorder.
Cyclothymic Disorder
Bipolar Disorder, NOS
Mood Disorder due to . . . a medical condition
Mood Disorder, NOS

All these disorders are considered to primarily have a chemical basis, and many have a genetic basis for their existence. When present, they can definitely interfere with one's ability to function and can certainly get in the way of any attempts to make changes in one's habits for the improvement of self-esteem.

I won't list the symptoms of all these disorders. I will look at the two most common—the depressive disorder of Major Depression and Dysthymic Disorder.

1. **Major Depression**: Five or more of the following symptoms must have been present during the same two-week period and represent a change from previous functioning. At least one of the symptoms has to be either depressed mood or loss of interest or pleasure. These symptoms include:
   - Depressed mood most of the day, nearly every day.
   - Markedly diminished interest or pleasure in all or almost all activities most of the day, nearly every day.
   - Significant weight loss when not dieting, or weight gain; i.e., a change of more than 5 percent of body weight in a month, or decrease or increase in appetite nearly every day.
   - Insomnia or hypersomnia nearly every day, i.e., reduced sleep or increased sleep as compared to normal sleep for the individual.
   - Psychomotor agitation, or retardation, nearly every day, i.e., mental/physical agitation or slowing.
   - Fatigue or loss of energy nearly every day.
   - Feelings of worthlessness or excessive or inappropriate guilt nearly every day.
   - Decreased ability to think or concentrate or indecisiveness nearly every day.
   - Recurrent thoughts of death. Recurrent suicidal ideation without a specific plan, or a suicide attempt, or a specific plan for committing suicide.

The symptoms involved have to cause clinically significant distress or impairment in functioning in areas of socializing, occupation or other important areas that cannot be due to the effects of a substance or medical condition, or usually the result of grief or bereavement.

2. **Dysthymic Disorder**: This kind of depression is a low-grade, chronic depression that many people have and are not even aware of. When they start to feel better, they then realize that the way they have been feeling for years actually has been abnormal and depressed. Criteria for dysthymia include the following:

   • There is a depressed mood for most of the day, for more days than not, that has been going on for at least two years.
   • While depressed, at least two of the following are also present:
     • Poor appetite or overeating.
     • Insomnia or hypersomnia.
     • Low energy or fatigue.
     • Low self-esteem.
     • Poor concentration or difficulty making decisions.
     • Feelings of hopelessness.

During the two-year period of the above symptoms, the person must have never been without the symptoms for greater than two months at a time. It is also important that these symptoms are not due to the direct effects of a substance or a general medical condition. Although there are more criteria in the DSM IV R regarding these diagnoses, the above, I feel, are the most important ones for you to consider as you look at your barriers to developing better "impressions of self."

APPENDIX B: ANXIETY DISORDERS

Anxiety is another very common psychiatric disorder that can severely interfere with functioning and one's ability to focus on and make changes in behaviors for the benefit of self-esteem. Again, according to the DSM IV-TR, there are several specific diagnoses under anxiety disorders. I will list those but will not give the symptoms of all of them. These different diagnoses include:

- Panic Disorder with or without agoraphobia.
- Agoraphobia without a history of panic disorder.
- A specific phobia such as being afraid of a particular animal or heights.
- Social phobia.
- Obsessive Compulsive Disorder.
- Post-traumatic Stress Disorder.
- Acute Stress Disorder.
- Generalized Anxiety Disorder.

- Anxiety Disorder due to something specific, such as a medical condition.
- Anxiety Disorder, NOS.

I want to look more specifically at two of these diagnostic criteria in terms of their symptoms.

1. **Panic Attack with or without agoraphobia**: This is defined as "a discrete period of intense fear or discomfort in which four of the following symptoms develop abruptly and reach the peak within 10 minutes."

- Palpitations, pounding heart or accelerated heart rate.
- Sweating.
- Trembling or shaking.
- Sensations or shortness of breath, or smothering.
- Feeling of chocking.
- Chest pain or discomfort.
- Nausea or abdominal distress.
- Feeling dizzy, unsteady, lightheaded or faint.
- Derealization [feelings of unreality] or depersonalization [being detached from one's self].
- Fear of losing control or going crazy.
- Fear of dying.
- Paresthesia [numbness or tingling sensations].
- Chills or hot flashes.

In terms of the agoraphobia part of this diagnosis, agoraphobia is noted to be a type of anxiety that occurs in regard to being in places or situations in which escape might be difficult [or embarrassing] or in which help may not be available in the event of having a panic attack or panic-like symptoms.

2. **Generalized Anxiety Disorder**: This is defined by the following symptoms.

- Excessive anxiety and worry about a number of events or activities, occurring more days than not for at least six months.
- The person finds it difficult to control the worry.
- The anxiety or worry is associated with three or more of the following six symptoms:
  - Restlessness or feeling keyed up or on edge.
  - Being easily fatigued.
  - Difficulty concentrating or mind going blank.
  - Irritability.
  - Muscle tension.
  - Sleep disturbance.

It is important that these symptoms are significant enough to cause distress or impairment in social, occupational or other important areas of functioning.

The disturbance is not due to the direct physiological effects of a substance or a general medical condition.

Again, I want to point out that the symptoms noted above are not the only ones to consider in making these diagnoses but are the main ones that I feel can help you identify these disorders if they are acting as a **barrier** to successfully working on self-esteem. If it is your impression that you meet the criteria in Appendix A or Appendix B, it would be appropriate to get a psychiatric evaluation. With such evaluation and possible treatment, the odds are strongly in your favor for getting rid of these **barriers**.

I realize that the thought of going to a psychiatrist can be uncomfortable. Years ago, such evaluation and treatment was mostly thought to be needed for psychotic people. That is far from the reality these days. We have learned a lot about psychiatric illnesses and about the abnormal neurochemistry that causes such illnesses as serious depression, anxiety, obsessive-compulsiveness, PTSD, schizophrenia, bipolar disorder, etc. They are truly medical illnesses or disorders. Thanks to this continuing research, more successful treatments are available. More people are realizing the need for treatment, and that getting treatment is okay. The majority of people I see are suffering from depression and/or anxiety and are still involved in everyday life.

ACKNOWLEDGEMENTS

I have a great deal of appreciation and thankfulness for all those who helped and supported me throughout the creation of this book.

I especially thank my family—my wife Lib for her giving of our time together to use for my writing and for her very helpful suggestions and editing, and especially for her continuing love and support; my son Chris and his artwork and time from his busy schedule to help me have a more visually pleasing presentation. I thank my daughters: Neicy Benge for her review and suggestions, and Julie Westin Mitchell and Jonie Roettjer Henriksson for helping with the multiple typing requirements. I am also grateful to several others who helped with typing over the years: Jonie Nelson, Judy Westin, Fiona Ferguson, Ima Sharp and Sybil Tiedemann. I am also grateful for the initial editing by Donna Breckenridge.

Very special thanks go to those who reviewed this manuscript and gave constructive feedback: Jack Marks, M.D.; John Racey, M.D.; Michael Myer, M.D.; Don Dickens; Judy McManus; and the Rev. Allen Breckenridge. Their comments, support, and suggestions were extremely helpful.

Thank you all,
Dennis